CONTENTS

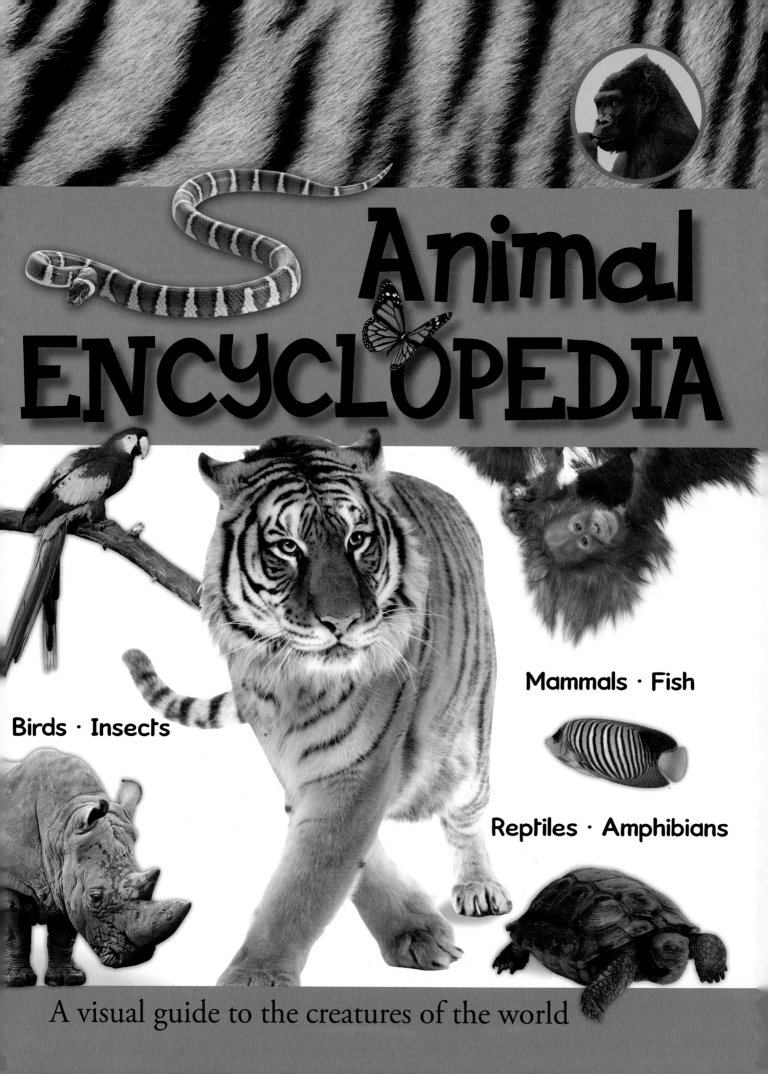

Animal ENCYCLOPEDIA

Mammals · Fish

Birds · Insects

Reptiles · Amphibians

A visual guide to the creatures of the world

CONTENTS

ABOUT ANIMALS

Animals are a large group of multi-cellular organisms. They are different from human beings. Animals can be divided into five groups: mammals, reptiles, amphibians, birds and fish.

Mammalia

There are more than 4,000 kinds of mammals in the world. They are warm-blooded animals and are found in all parts of the world. They are the most intelligent creatures on earth and can **adapt** their body temperature to different climatic conditions and temperatures.

Some amphibians begin their life in the water. Frogs for example begin their life as tadpoles in the water.

Amphibians and Reptiles

Both amphibians and reptiles are cold-blooded animals that breathe through lungs. Amphibians, however, can also live underwater. Frogs and toads are amphibians while snakes and lizards are called reptiles.

Kangaroos belong to a class of mammals known as marsupials.

In Air and in Water

Birds are warm-blooded animals that lay eggs. Unlike other animals, birds can fly using wings. However, there are some birds, like the ostrich, that do not fly. Fish, on the other hand, stay only in water. They will die if they are taken out of water. They breathe through **gills**.

CANINES

Canine (or Canidae) is the name for the dog family that includes wolves, foxes, coyotes and jackals. There are about 400 species of dog in the world.

The Fox

The fox is the most common mammal found in the world. It is much smaller than other canines. The fox is also a solitary animal, unlike many other canines that live in groups. The red fox is the most common species.

The sandy coloured coat of the Fennec fox allows it to blend into the desert surroundings.

A fox's large ears help to dissipate heat and detect movement.

Fun Facts

The Arctic fox is the only member of the Canidae family that changes the colour of its coat according to the season. While its winter coat is white, it has a bluish grey coat in summer.

The Fennec fox is the smallest fox in the world.

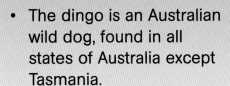

- The dingo is an Australian wild dog, found in all states of Australia except Tasmania.

- Wolves have two layers of fur. The first layer helps to repel water and dust while the second layer helps to keep the body warm.

- Fox hunting began as a sport in the 16th century in the UK.

Wolves

Wolves belong to the same family as domesticated dogs. They are found in remote forests and hunt in packs. They feed on large and medium-sized animals like sheep, pigs and deer. There are two main species of wolves - the red and the grey.

Grey wolves are the largest Canines.

DID YOU KNOW?

Foxes store their food under leaves, snow or soil to eat later.

BIG CATS

The big cats are the largest members of the cat family and include tigers, lions, leopards and jaguars. They are distinguished by their ability to roar.

The Striped Prowler

The tiger is the largest member of the big cat family. They grow up to 4 m (13 ft) in length and weigh over 300 kg (660 lbs). They are **nocturnal** animals and hunt for their prey at night. They have strong eyesight and a keen sense of smell. There are five different species of tiger in the world.

The Royal Bengal tiger is found in the rainforests and grasslands of Bangladesh, Bhutan, Burma, China, India and Nepal.

The Royal Bengal tiger has orange and white fur with black stripes.

Second in Charge

The lion is the second largest living cat. Unlike other big cats, lions live in big groups of about 15 animals, known as a pride. Male lions are recognised by the thick mane of brown hair that encircles their head and neck.

Lions are the most social of the big cats, living in groups.

- Though the leopard is the smallest member of the big cat family, it is still the best and strongest climber of all the large cats.

- The Siberian tiger (also known as the Amur) is a rare species of the tiger family. Only 7,000 Siberians are left in the world today.

- Cougars, also known as panthers or pumas, are the largest cats that can purr!

Fun Facts

Tigers have more than a hundred stripes on their body but no two tigers have the same number and pattern of stripes.

DID YOU KNOW?

Lions are the laziest of all the big cats. They sleep and rest for more than 20 hours a day!

HOOVED ANIMALS

Hooved animals are also known as ungulates. They can be odd-toed or even-toed, depending on the number of toes.

The camel's large nostrils store water vapour and help prevent water loss.

Fun Facts

All camels have a very unique stomach. Unlike humans or other animals, their stomachs are divided into three compartments, helping them in the digestion of their food.

Ship of the Desert

Most camels live in the desert, but some species are found in other arid areas like mountains. They can survive for a long time without water. Their **hump** is made of fatty tissues, which helps them control their body temperature and also act as an energy reserve to help them withstand long periods of heat and dehydration.

- The wild bactrian camel is one of the rarest mammals in the world.

- Camel meat is very healthy since it has no cholesterol and very little fat.

- Oryx antelopes, found in deserts, have a unique system of cooling their blood before it reaches their brain. This helps them regulate their body temperature to cope with living in hot, dry conditions.

Antelopes often have large horns that spiral up from their head.

Deer horns are different from the antelope's; they can shed their antlers, which then grow again.

Hooving Around

Antelopes are hooved mammals with hollow horns. They can be found in a variety of habitats. However, most of them live in grasslands. Antelope horns are made of a hard substance called keratin and grow throughout their lives.

DID YOU KNOW?

Camels were used by the Bedouins in war against the Persians in the 7th century B.C.

MONKEYS AND APES

Monkeys and apes are mammals. They belong to the same category that human beings are a part of – **primates.**

Orangutans are apes that live in the rainforests of Borneo and Sumatra.

Their Habitat

Monkeys are found in many types of habitat – from forests and deserts to grasslands and mountains. They are found in all parts of the world. Apes, however, live only in the rainforests of Africa and Asia.

A group of monkeys is called a troop.

Fun Facts

Chimpanzees have a cheeky trick of poking a long stick into an ant hill. When the ants have crawled onto the stick, the chimpanzee takes the stick out and licks up all the ants!

Some monkeys have long tails that help them hold on to branches as they swing between trees.

Their Differences

Monkeys are different from apes in many ways. Most monkeys have tails but apes do not have tails. Apes can use their hands to swing from branch to branch. Monkeys cannot do that. Instead, they run on the tree branches.

- A monkey's eyes are rounder and closer together than human eyes.
- In some monkeys, the arms are as long as the legs.
- Monkeys do not catch a cold!
- Experts say that vervet monkeys have their own language.

A male gorilla is more than ten times stronger than an average adult man.

Male gorillas typically have a patch of silver hair on their back.

Gorillas walk on all four limbs, putting pressure on their knuckles. This is called knuckle-walking.

DID YOU KNOW?

Monkeys eat bananas just like us. They first peel off the skin and then eat the fruit.

15

ELEPHANTS

Elephants are the largest living land animals. They live in secluded areas, far from human beings.

Trunking Around

Elephants weigh between 90-120 kg (200-265 lbs) when they are born. Elephants live in small groups. They eat roots, bark, grass, leaves and fruit. They have been known to uproot entire trees to reach the fruit!

Close Cousins

The Asian elephant is smaller than its African counterpart and has smaller ears. Despite their weight, elephants walk very quietly, distributing their weight by a thick cushion of tissue on the base of their foot.

When travelling, elephants move in a single file.

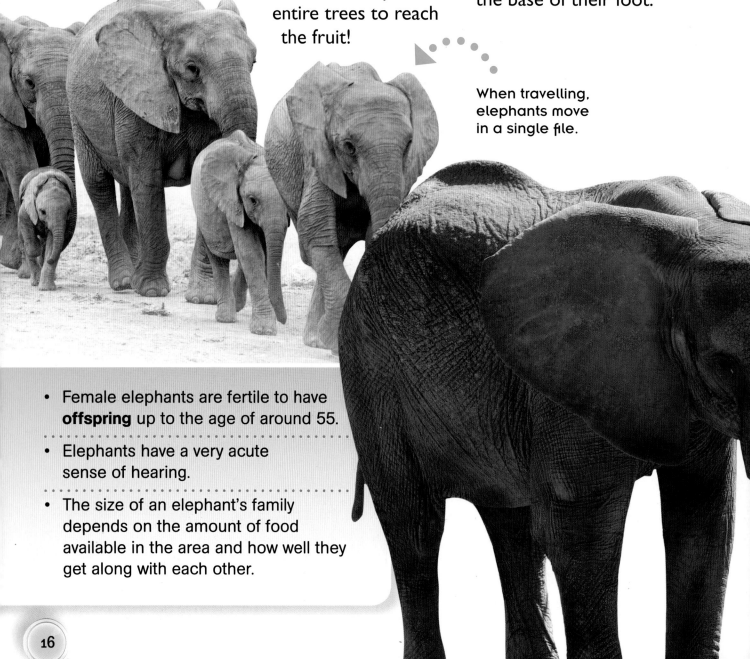

- Female elephants are fertile to have **offspring** up to the age of around 55.
- Elephants have a very acute sense of hearing.
- The size of an elephant's family depends on the amount of food available in the area and how well they get along with each other.

RHINOS AND HIPPOS

Rhinoceroses and hippopotamuses are also classified as ungulates or hooved animals. The hippo lives on riverbanks. The rhino has horns.

Horned Nose

Rhinos are huge, with most species weighing nearly one tonne! They have a large horn above the nose and a tough exterior skin between 1.5-5 cm (0.5-2 in) thick. There are five types of rhinos: white, black, Indian, Sumatran and Javan.

The rhino's horn is made of keratin and was traditionally used in Asian medicines.

Fun Facts

Even when a hippo is sleeping underwater, it raises its head to breathe without even waking up!

River Horse

The hippo (literally meaning 'river horse') spends its days in water and comes to the land at night to eat. A hippo can spend long periods underwater, but typically surfaces every 3 to 5 minutes to breathe. They are native to Africa.

- Hippos often scare away their **predator**s by opening their mouth and showing their canines, which can grow up to 50 cm (20 in) in length.
- The Javan rhino is one of the rarest and most **endangered** animal in the world.
- Hippos secrete a red substance from their skin, which acts like a natural sunscreen.

BEARS

Bears are solitary animals, usually active in the early morning or at dusk. Bears are usually found in parts of the Americas, Europe and Asia.

The grizzly bear, like other brown bears, can be distinguished by the hump on its back, made up of muscle. This bundle of muscles gives the bear the force to dig its forelimbs into its prey.

Bears are good at climbing trees and are great swimmers.

The Big Brown Bear

The brown bear can be found all over Europe, Asia and North America. Despite its name, some species can be brown, black and even blonde. Brown bears are very powerful animals and can break the necks of even large prey when they hunt.

Fun Facts

Hibernating female bears don't even wake up when they give birth to their cubs during winter. The baby bear cubs crawl into a position where they can feed themselves from their mother soon after birth.

White as Snow

Polar bears live around the Arctic Ocean. They have a thick layer of fat under their skin, which helps them keep warm in cold climates and also helps them float while swimming. They also have two layers of fur.

- While the brown bear, the black bear and the panda rely on fruit, nuts and berries as their primary source of food, it is only the Polar bear that is mainly carnivorous in nature, feeding on seals.

- Pandas do not hibernate like other species of bears

- The grizzly bear is the largest meat eater in the world.

Despite their size, bears are fast runners.

The Polar bear lives mainly on seal meat.

The grizzly bear gets its name from the grey or silver tips of the hair on its back.

DID YOU KNOW?

Brown bears eat almost continuously during the summer and autumn as they get ready for winter.

RODENTS

Rodents are the largest order of mammals in terms of number of species. They have sharp incisor teeth that grow continuously and must be kept short by gnawing. They are found everywhere except in Antarctica.

Notorious Nibblers

Mice are the most common rodents and are found across the world. They typically prefer seeds and grains. They can also survive for long periods of time with little or no water, obtaining their water from the food that they eat. They are mainly nocturnal animals.

- Hamsters are named after the German word, *hamstern*, which means to hoard. This is due to the fact that these creatures carry food in their cheek pouches and hide it away safely.

- Pet gerbils have to be provided with things they can chew to prevent their very sharp incisors from growing too long.

Mice are usually most active at night.

Gentle Guinea Pigs

Small rodents like hamsters, gerbils and guinea pigs have become popular as family pets. Guinea pigs are the largest of all pet rodents. They are considered to be very good pets and seldom bite or scratch even if stressed or disturbed. They vary widely in hair composition and colour. Some have a smooth coat while others have a ruffled coat.

Fun Facts

Guinea pigs jump excitedly when threatened. This movement is known as 'pop corning' and is a type of war dance to scare away predators and escape to safety.

The capybara is the world's largest rodent. It can grow as big as a dog.

If guinea pigs don't get food to chew on, they chew on their own hair or even on plastic or cloth.

Their mild nature makes guinea pigs very popular as pets.

DID YOU KNOW?

Millions of people died in Europe in the 14th century because of a terrible disease carried by rats and transmitted by fleas. This was known as the Black Death.

BIRDS

Birds are warm-blooded vertebrates that lay eggs. There are more than 10,000 living species of birds in the world. All birds have feathers, beaks and wings, but not all can fly.

Diet

While most birds are plant eating creatures, there are some birds that are meat eating. These are known as raptors or birds of prey. Vultures, hawks, eagles and kites are all birds of prey.

Most birds are active in the day. However, some birds like the owl are active at night.

Fly Away

Flying allows birds to travel, hunt for food and avoid predators. Birds have a very light skeleton, strong flying muscles and wings. The shape and size of the wing determines the distance and type of flight for birds. Feathers provide insulation and help maintain body temperature.

Songbirds

Birds that have musical voices are called songbirds. They have specially developed vocal cords or syringes, which they use to produce sounds or 'songs'. They also have a special section in their brain which helps them learn their songs.

FLIGHTLESS BIRDS

While most birds can fly, there are some birds that do not fly. Even though they look like birds, their legs are adapted in many instances to help them cover long distances by walking or running.

A kiwi may be the size of a chicken, but its egg is up to six times larger than a chicken's!

Running Bird

The ostrich is the largest flightless bird in the world. Found in parts of Africa, they weigh 113-181 kg (250-400 lbs) and stand 1.8-2.4 m (6-8 ft) tall. They have two-toed feet that allow them to run fast and escape from predators.

New Zealander

The kiwi is also a flightless bird. This protected and endangered national bird of New Zealand is nocturnal by nature. The kiwi's beak is almost one-third the length of its body. It uses its excellent sense of smell to hunt for worms, insects, berries and seeds.

The long neck of the ostrich gives it the ability to see a greater distance across the plains.

- To produce her huge egg, the female kiwi must eat three times her normal food intake for a month!

- Emus, like the ostrich, drink large quantities of water and can drink up to 70 mouthfuls of water at one go.

- Contrary to popular belief, ostriches do not bury their head in the sand when they see danger.

DID YOU KNOW?

Emu eggs are dark green in colour. Each egg can weigh up to 0.68 kgs (1.5 lbs).

REPTILES

Reptiles are cold-blooded animals and are covered with scales or plates, as apposed to skin or feathers. The majority of reptiles are **oviparous**, meaning they lay eggs, from which their young are born.

- Four main orders of reptiles are recognised: **Crocodilia** (including crocodiles and alligators); **Sphenodontia** (including tuatara); **Squamata** (including lizards and snakes); **Testudines** (including turtles and tortoises).

- Most reptiles lay eggs, but some lizards and snakes give birth to live young.

- The horned lizard is known to defend itself from its enemies by spraying them with blood from the corner of its eye.

Slithering Around

Lizards make up the largest group of reptiles. There are over 3,700 species of lizards spread all over the world. Lizards also have dry, scaly skin and clawed feet. They usually feed on insects, with some being vegetarians.

Komodo dragons can eat up to 80 per cent of their body weight during a single meal.

The Komodo dragon is the largest lizard in the world.

The mouth of the Komodo dragon is full of poisonous bacteria capable of killing a man.

Mobile Homes

Turtles are also classified as reptiles. They have a hard shell on their back that acts like armour. Most turtles live in the sea. Turtles also have a beak but do not have any teeth. Their hard jaw rim helps them cut and chew food. Tortoises also belong to the same family as turtles but live on land.

Tortoises can draw their head, legs and tails into their hard shell when they sense danger.

Fun Facts

The average life span of a common snapping turtle is about 40 years. However, the giant tortoise is known to live for as long as 170 years!

DID YOU KNOW?

Chameleons have an amazing ability to change the colour of their body instantly.

SNAKES

Snakes are also reptiles, but they do not have legs. They are cold-blooded and usually nocturnal in nature. Some species, however, can be found in the day.

Slithering Around

Snakes do not have external ears but can sense sound through **vibrations**. They have an inner ear and can feel the vibrations on the ground. The vibration is then passed onto the inner ear and helps them hunt. They also have smell sensors on the tips of their tongues and heat sensors, which help them in locating food.

Some snakes have a flap of skin on the side of their head. These flare out to form a hood and help scare predators away.

Fun Facts

Snakes do not hear a snake charmer. When we see a snake swaying to the music of the snake charmer it is actually moving to the vibrations of the charmer's movement.

Snakes have a transparent scale that covers the eye. The scale is frequently replaced by a new one helping the snake see clearly again.

Snakes have a flexible lower jaw that helps them swallow their prey whole.

Snakes use their nostrils only for breathing. They smell with their tongues.

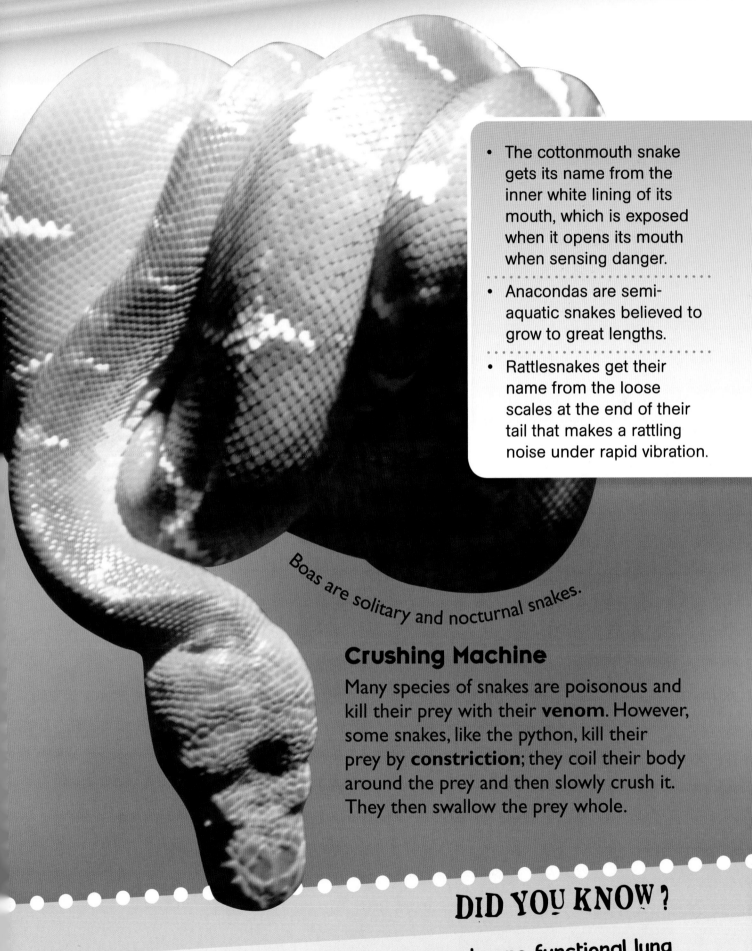

- The cottonmouth snake gets its name from the inner white lining of its mouth, which is exposed when it opens its mouth when sensing danger.

- Anacondas are semi-aquatic snakes believed to grow to great lengths.

- Rattlesnakes get their name from the loose scales at the end of their tail that makes a rattling noise under rapid vibration.

Boas are solitary and nocturnal snakes.

Crushing Machine

Many species of snakes are poisonous and kill their prey with their **venom**. However, some snakes, like the python, kill their prey by **constriction**; they coil their body around the prey and then slowly crush it. They then swallow the prey whole.

DID YOU KNOW?

Snakes have only one functional lung located on the right side of their body.

AMPHIBIANS

Amphibians can live on both land and in water. Most amphibians begin their life in water. Even fully grown, they cannot live all their life on land.

In Land and Water

Frogs, toads, and salamanders are all types of amphibians. Most amphibians are born in water, where the eggs are laid. Amphibians that are spawned in water do not have limbs and look more like fish. They breathe through gills and have tails to help them swim. Over time, their lungs and legs grow in a process known as **metamorphosis**.

A newt is a salamander that lives in the water as an adult.

Fun Facts

Most frogs live in and around water. However, there are also some types of frogs that never go near water and live only on land and even on trees, extracting moisture from the air!

There are more than 6,000 species of amphibians in the world.

Frog Story

Frogs are found in most parts of the world. Almost all species of frogs have long back legs and shorter front legs, which help them to move. Frogs are usually green in colour, but many also have colourful markings on their body.

Most frogs have large bulging eyes.

The skin of frogs has the ability to absorb water.

- Salamanders are short-legged amphibians, usually with long tails.

- Newts are a type of salamander and may be fully- or semi-aquatic.

- Frogs catch live prey by darting out their long, sticky tongue. The marine toad eats plants as well as scavenged flesh.

Their strong back legs help frogs leap to safety whenever they sense danger.

DID YOU KNOW?

Some rainforest frogs are very poisonous. This poison has traditionally been used to tip arrows and darts.

SHARKS AND RAYS

The great white shark is the most feared of all sharks.

Sharks and rays are among some of the most feared and misunderstood creatures in the seas and oceans.

Sharks use their tail to provide thrust and speed while swimming.

The whale shark is the largest shark. It is also the largest fish in the world and can grow up to 15 m (50 ft) long!

Predators at Sea

Sharks are a type of fish. They do not have bones like other fish but are made up of cartilage – strong tissue as hard as bone. Sharks have a keen sense of smell and some can detect just a drop of blood from quite a distance. Many sharks also have keen eyesight.

Poisonous Sting

Stingrays are related to sharks and get their name from the **serrated**, poisonous spine that grows from their tail. Stingrays can grow as long as 4.6 m (15 ft). However, they normally only sting only in **self defence**.

Stingrays spend most of their time inactive, buried in the sand on the ocean floor.

- Stingrays are a family of fish and include several different species.

- There are about 368 species of sharks in the world.

- Some shark species are **oviparous** (egg-layers) and some are **viviparous**, giving birth to live pups.

CRABS AND SHELLFISH

Crustacea and molluscs are another type of marine life. They include crabs, lobsters, shrimps, and crayfish. The octopus is a type of mollusc.

Crustacea

The crab and the lobster are some of the most popular crustacea in the world. They have a soft inner body and a hard outer shell called an **exoskeleton**. The shell does not grow in size; rather, the outer shell is shed at regular intervals as a larger shell develops beneath.

Prey Suckers

The octopus is an invertebrate with a bag-shaped body, a large head and eight tentacles used to catch prey. Octopuses have the remarkable ability to change both the colour and the texture of their body. This helps them to merge into their surroundings and escape from enemies. Snails and slugs also belong to the same family as the octopus.

The octopus squirts out a black inky substance when it is threatened. It uses the resulting cloud to make its escape.

The horseshoe crab has changed very little in over 25 million years.

A crab's claws are known as chelae.

31

MARINE MAMMALS

There are about 120 species of mammals in the world that can be classified as marine mammals, including whales, dolphins and walruses.

A whale's tail fin is horizontal and not vertical like a shark's.

Whales

Whales are among the biggest living creatures in the world. Whales are warm-blooded and give birth to live young. They breathe air through lungs and have to surface at regular intervals to breathe in through blowholes situated on top of their heads. Baleen whales have a sieve-like structure, which they use to separate plankton from the water. The toothed whales have teeth and eat fish and squid.

- Dolphins and whales use sound waves to locate their food and other objects in the water.
- The killer whale (orca) is actually the largest dolphin and can grow up to 6.1 m (20 ft) long.
- The average bottlenose dolphin brain weighs 1.5 kgs (3.4 lbs) more than the human brain.

Dolphins

Dolphins belong to the same family (**cetaceans**) as whales but are physically different from them. They can be found in all oceans and seas and feed on small fish, squid, crabs, shrimps and lobsters. Dolphins are also social animals and live in large groups of 12 or more animals. These groups are known as pods.

Seals and Walruses

Walruses and seals are flippered mammals and belong to the family of pinnipeds. Walruses live in the Arctic Ocean and sub-Arctic seas of the Northern Hemisphere. Seals live in the Antarctic region.

Although they live in saltwater, dolphins do not drink water. They get their water from their food.

Dolphins are playful creatures, often racing through the water and jumping out of it.

Fun Facts

Dolphins have to be conscious to breath, meaning they can never fall asleep completely. Instead, they let one half of their brain sleep at a time.

DID YOU KNOW ?

Dolphins can produce unique whistles that help individual dolphins recognise each other.

SPIDERS AND SCORPIONS

Spiders and scorpions belong to the family of arachnids. There are over 100,000 species of arachnids in the world. They are different from insects in many ways, including having eight legs instead of six.

Web Masters

Spiders are found in all parts of the world and in every kind of habitat. They can be found in many colours. They are carnivores and hunt their prey through their sticky webs or by other clever traps.

Most spiders are extremely sensitive to sound and vibrations.

Spiders do not have claws but some have poisonous fangs.

The body of a spider is divided into two main parts, the thorax and abdomen.

Not all spiders are a dull black or brown.

Fun Facts

Some spiders have stripes and blotches on their body. This is a technique called *disruptive colouration* and helps them merge into the background and escape from predators.

- Scorpions usually eat insects. When food is scarce they have the amazing ability to slow down their metabolism and eat one third their normal amount of food.

- Though scorpions can live without food and even in harsh conditions, they cannot survive in areas where there is no loose soil.

- The jumping spider gets more than 90 per cent of its food from solid plant material produced by acacias.

Pincer Attack

Scorpions are closely related to spiders, mites and ticks. Scorpions are found in deserts, in the Brazilian rainforests and even the Himalayan mountains! Most scorpions are nocturnal by nature and (contrary to popular belief) are not aggressive towards humans, unless provoked!

Scorpions navigate using sensory hairs and slit organs on their legs.

DID YOU KNOW?

There are almost 2,000 species of scorpions but only 30-40 species are poisonous enough to kill a human.

CREEPY CRAWLIES

Insects make up the largest group of creatures on earth. Eight out of every ten of all species are insects!

Hard Life

Insects are **arthropods**, meaning they have joint legs and a tough cover known as an exoskeleton outside their body. Confusingly, all insects are arthropods but not all arthropods are insects! The hard exoskeleton supports the body of the insect and helps protect the soft inner parts.

Parts and More

Most insects are born as eggs and grow into a larva, called a nymph. The larva becomes a pupa before becoming an adult. An insect's body consists of the head, thorax and abdomen. The head has a pair of antennae, eyes and a mouth. The thorax supports the legs and wings while the abdomen helps digest food.

- Insects that live in large colonies are known as social insects. Ants and bees are social insects.
- Different insects lay their eggs in different places. While some lay their eggs inside plant stems, some insects, like the beetle, lay their eggs on dead animals.
- Some insects, including mosquitos, lice and bedbugs are known as pests. However, there are some that are helpful to us, such as bees.

A queen bee can lay over 1,000 eggs in a day.

While some insects have simple eyes, most have compound eyes consisting of six-sided lenses.

The EARTH

Creation · Structure

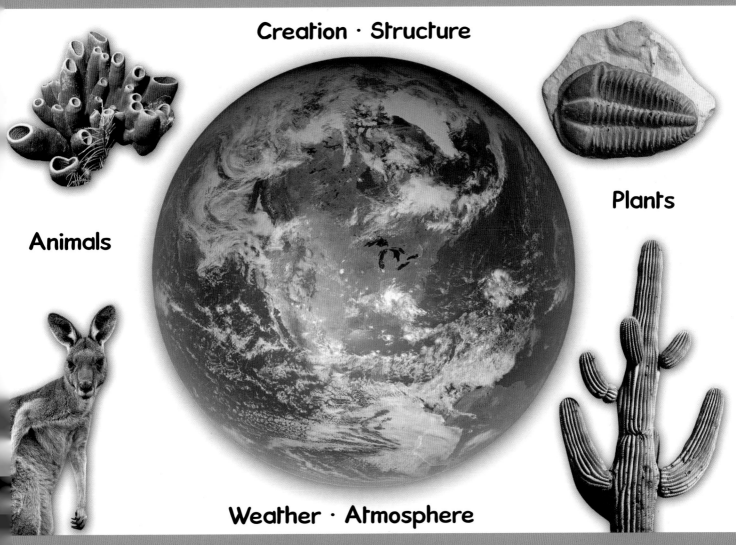

Animals

Plants

Weather · Atmosphere

A visual guide to our amazing planet

THE EARTH'S BEGINNING

No one really understands how the **Universe** came to be. Most scientists believe it all started around **14,000 million years ago**, with a giant explosion called the **Big Bang**.

The **Big Bang** created a giant fireball, which cooled and expanded, forming tiny particles called **matter**.

As the particles spread out, the Universe began to grow, and thick clouds of hydrogen and helium gases formed. Over time, these clouds joined together to make dense clusters, which eventually formed the first galaxies.

Some 10,000 million years after the Big Bang, our **Sun** and the **planets** of our **Solar System** formed in a **spiral galaxy** called the **Milky Way.**

Fun Facts

From 1930 Pluto was believed to be the ninth planet of our Solar System. In 2006, Pluto was removed from the list for being too small. It is now called a dwarf planet or a Kuiper Belt Object.

Each planet has a fixed path around the Sun. Right next to the Sun is Mercury. Then comes Venus, Earth, Mars, Jupiter, Saturn, Uranus and, finally, Neptune.

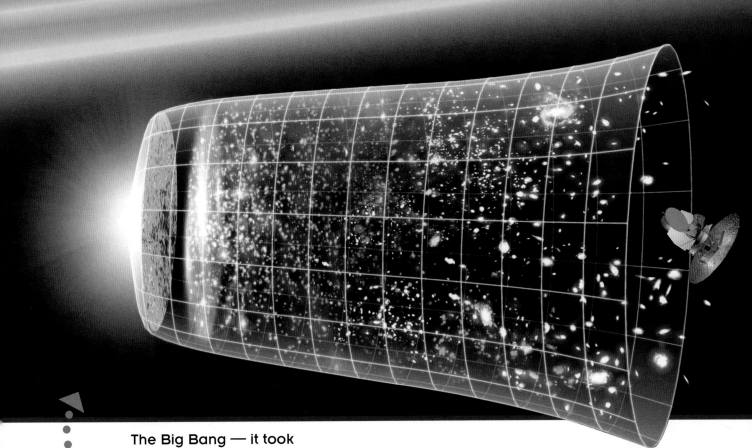

The Big Bang — it took less than a second and the universe was formed.

The **Earth orbits the Sun** at a distance of **149.6 million kilometres**, which makes it just the right temperature for **water** to exist as a **liquid**, as well as in solid form (**ice**), and as a **vapour**.

The Earth also has a **breathable atmosphere**, which, when viewed from space, looks like a very thin blue layer surrounding our planet.

These characteristics mean that the Earth, unlike any of the other planets in our Solar System, is able to **support life**.

- The name "Earth" is at least 1,000 years old. All the other planets are named after Greek & Roman Goddesses. "Earth" is an English/German word which simply means "ground".

- Though the planet is called Earth, only about thirty per cent of its surface is actually 'earth'. The rest is water!

Did You Know ?

In one second, the Earth travels about 30 km (19 miles) around the Sun.

THE STRUCTURE OF THE EARTH

The Earth is made up of different layers, which formed when the planet was young, and extremely hot.

These layers are all held in place by the enormous force of **gravity** acting upon the planet's **inner core**, an incredibly hot ball of **iron** and **nickel**.

Some of the layers are partly **molten**, which means that they contain extremely hot liquid, and are covered by an outer layer of **solid rock**, called the **crust**.

The rock that makes up the surface of the Earth is constantly changing as more and more layers are added. Its composition can be divided into three different types of rock:

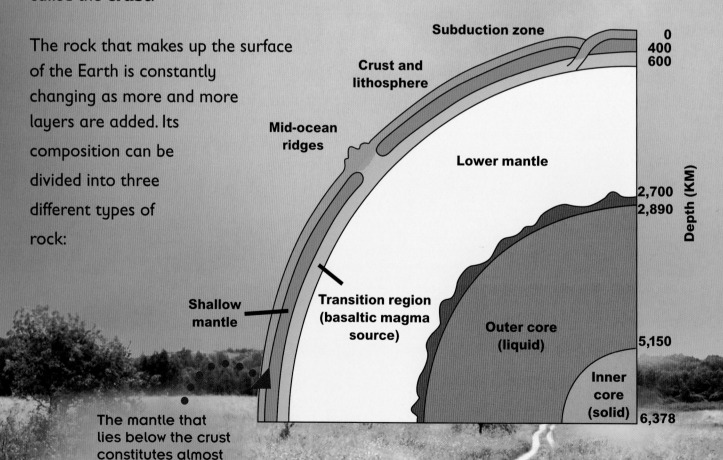

Subduction zone

Crust and lithosphere

Mid-ocean ridges

Lower mantle

Shallow mantle

Transition region (basaltic magma source)

Outer core (liquid)

Inner core (solid)

Depth (KM)

0
400
600

2,700
2,890

5,150

6,378

The mantle that lies below the crust constitutes almost two-thirds of the Earth's mass.

Igneous rock is formed when **molten** rock cools and becomes solid.

Sedimentary rock is formed when **sediments** (such as rock particles) are deposited by water, buried, and squashed into layers called **strata**.

Metamorphic rock is formed when existing rock is changed from its original form by intense **heat** or **pressure**.

The Earth's crust is thickest below the continents.

Crust: Temperature: Around 22°C. **State**: Solid. **Composition**: Oceanic crust made up of iron, oxygen, silicon, magnesium, and aluminium. Continental crust is made up of granite, sedimentary rocks, and metamorphic rocks.

Upper Mantle: Temperature: 1,400°C – 3,000°C. **State**: Solid and melted (liquid) rock. **Composition**: Iron, oxygen, silicon, magnesium, and aluminium

Lower Mantle: Temperature: 3,000°C. **State**: Solid. **Composition**: Iron, oxygen, silicon, magnesium, and aluminium.

Inner Core: Temperature: 4,000°C – 6,000°C. **State**: Liquid. **Composition**: Iron, nickel, sulphur, and oxygen.

Outer Core: Temperature: 5,000°C - 6,000°C. **State**: Solid. **Composition**: Iron and nickel.

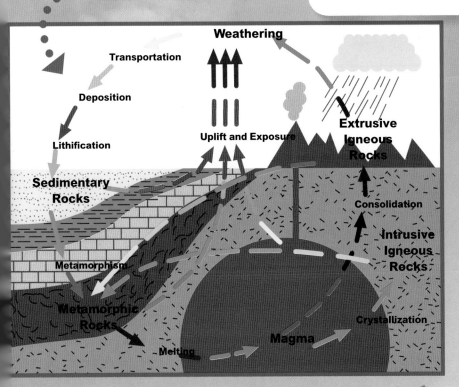

The structural secrets buried deep inside the Earth are revealed through the study of **seismic waves**, which are caused by earthquakes, explosions, and the movements of our oceans.

There are two different types of seismic wave: **shear waves**, which cannot travel through liquids, and **pressure waves**, which are able to move through both liquids and solids. These waves show that the Earth is made up of five different layers, all of varying thicknesses or **densities**.

Did You Know?

Estimates of the temperature of the Earth's inner core vary, but scientists believe it is probably between 5,000 - 7,000°C (9,000 - 13,000°F).

THE SURFACE OF THE EARTH

The thickness of the Earth's crust varies from between **5 kilometres** and **70 kilometres**. Thicker, **continental crust** forms the land, and thinner, **oceanic crust** makes up the ocean floors.

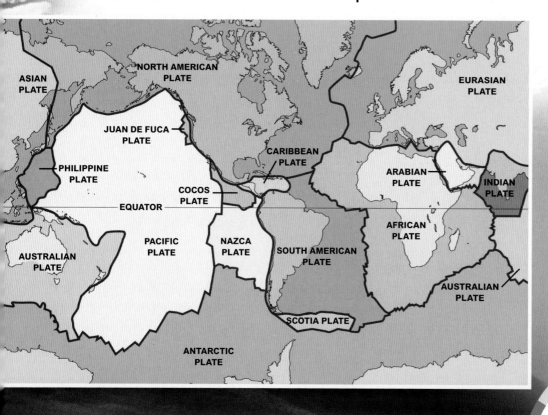

ASIAN PLATE

NORTH AMERICAN PLATE

JUAN DE FUCA PLATE

PHILIPPINE PLATE

COCOS PLATE

EQUATOR

CARIBBEAN PLATE

EURASIAN PLATE

ARABIAN PLATE

INDIAN PLATE

AFRICAN PLATE

PACIFIC PLATE

NAZCA PLATE

SOUTH AMERICAN PLATE

AUSTRALIAN PLATE

AUSTRALIAN PLATE

SCOTIA PLATE

ANTARCTIC PLATE

The Crust

The crust is broken into irregular **plates**, which drift over the **upper mantle** layer near the Earth's surface.

Always on the Move

We use the word **"tectonics"** to describe the movement of these plates: some slide past one another, while others come together, and still others drift apart.

Because all the Earth's plates fit together like a giant jigsaw puzzle, the movement of one plate affects the others all around it.

Fun Facts

The first landmasses appeared soon after the Earth was formed. They moved, joined together, and broke apart many times throughout the planet's history.

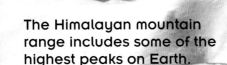
The Himalayan mountain range includes some of the highest peaks on Earth.

Fascinating Features

Many of the Earth's most fascinating features occur at **plate boundaries**, where different plates meet. **Mountain ranges**, for example, are formed when two **continental plates collide**.

Volcanoes, ocean trenches, and **earthquakes** are all the result of the movement of the Earth's plates.

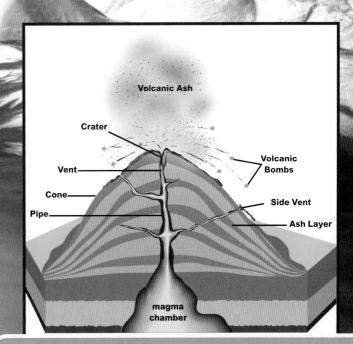

Volcanic Ash

Crater

Vent

Cone

Pipe

Volcanic Bombs

Side Vent

Ash Layer

magma chamber

- The movement of the liquid outer core is believed to create the Earth's magnetic field. This field creates two poles called magnetic North and Magnetic South.

- Around 250 million years ago there was just one massive landmass called Pangaea.

Did You Know?

225 million years ago, Pangaea started to divide, and the continents we know today began to form.

MOUNTAINS

When plates on the ocean floor move apart, **magma** from the Earth's **mantle** wells up along the boundary. Over time, the magma cools and hardens, forming a **mountain range** or **ridge** of new crust.

Spreading ridges occur as the movement continues, and more magma wells up along the centre of the existing ridge.

A boundary where a new crust is formed is called a **constructive boundary**.

Destructive boundaries, or **subduction zones**, occur where one plate is forced beneath another, and begins to melt.

Sometimes, two plates push together above the ground, causing the Earth's crust to buckle and fold upwards. These movements form high mountain ranges called **fold mountains**.

It is near impossible to live in freezing Antarctica.

Mount Everest, in the Himalayas, is the tallest mountain on Earth above sea level.

If you measure the height of mountains from the centre of the Earth, however, Everest wouldn't even get into the highest 20!

This is because the Earth isn't a perfect sphere - it is slightly squashed, and bulges out in the middle, giving an advantage to mountains situated along the equator.

The world's highest unclimbed mountain is Gangkhar Puensum in Bhutan, which is the 40th highest mountain in the world.

Due to the tectonic plate movement, Everest grows about 4mm every year.

Fun Facts

The oldest person ever to climb Everest is Yuichiro Miura of Japan, who was 80 years old at the time of his climb!

Did You Know ?

Chimborazo, in Ecuador, is actually the highest mountain in the world, and the closest to space, when measured from the centre of the Earth, because of the planet's strange shape!

THE EARTH'S ATMOSPHERE

Our planet is surrounded by a blanket of gases called the **atmosphere**, which is held in place by **gravity**, and makes it possible for living things to survive on Earth.

Viewed from space, the atmosphere looks like a thin blue haze, because of the way in which sunlight is filtered through the **atmospheric gases**.

It is these gases that enable living things to **breathe** the air around them. They also act as a shield, protecting us from the Sun's harmful **ultraviolet rays**.

The early atmosphere would have been **poisonous** to living things.

A breathable atmosphere only began to form when the first **plant-like organisms** appeared in the Earth's oceans. They used **light** from the **Sun** to make food from **water** and **carbon-dioxide**, releasing **oxygen** into the air as a by-product.

Millions of years later, enough oxygen had collected in the Earth's atmosphere to support new, more complex life forms.

Burning **fuels** and **forests** has released lots of extra **carbon dioxide** into the atmosphere, which has built up over time, trapping the Sun's heat around the Earth. This is known as the **greenhouse effect,** and is likely to cause **global warming**.

Fun Facts

If you went soaring through the atmosphere in a hot air balloon, you would find it harder to breathe the higher you went as the atmosphere got thinner!

Troposphere: The troposphere begins at the surface of the Earth and extends upwards by around 8 to 14.5 kilometres (5 to 9 miles). This part of the atmosphere is the most dense. Almost all weather occurs in this region.

Stratosphere: This layer begins just above the troposphere and extends for a further 50 kilometers (31 miles). The ozone layer, which absorbs and scatters ultraviolet radiation from the Sun, is in this layer.

Mesosphere: Meteors burn up in the mesosphere, which starts just above the stratosphere and extends up to 85 kilometers (53 miles) high.

Thermosphere: Aurora and satellites occur in the thermosphere layer, which begins just above the mesosphere and extends 600 kilometers (372 miles).

Ionosphere: The ionosphere grows and shrinks according to solar conditions and can be divided into further sub-regions. It contains a high concentration of electrons and ionized atoms, and is able to reflect radio waves. This region is what makes radio communications possible.

Exosphere: This is the outermost limit of the Earth's atmosphere. It extends from the top of the thermosphere to around 10,000 km (6,200 mi) high.

Layered like an Onion!

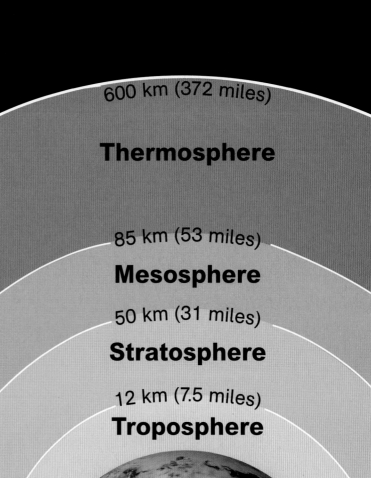

600 km (372 miles)

Thermosphere

85 km (53 miles)

Mesosphere

50 km (31 miles)

Stratosphere

12 km (7.5 miles)

Troposphere

The troposphere is where you find life on Earth.

Did You Know?

The mixture of gases in the atmosphere has taken over 4.5 billion years to evolve! Around 99% of the atmosphere is made up of oxygen and nitrogen. The remainder is tiny amounts of other gases.

LIFE ON EARTH

Living things need just the right amounts of **heat** and **light** from the **Sun**, as well as **food**, **water**, and **oxygen** to survive.

The Earth is the only planet in our **Solar System** known to support life, and it has taken millions and millions of years for conditions on our planet to become suitable for the plants and animals living here today.

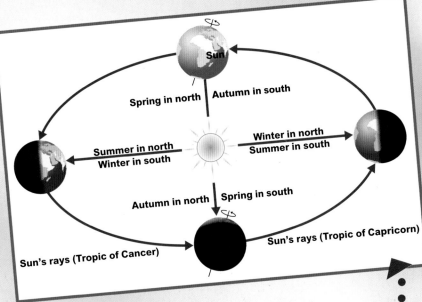

Sun

Spring in north   Autumn in south

Summer in north   Winter in north
Winter in south   Summer in south

Autumn in north   Spring in south

Sun's rays (Tropic of Cancer)   Sun's rays (Tropic of Capricorn)

The Earth going around the Sun.

Population

We use the word "**population**" to describe all the people living in a particular place. The world's population is greater today than ever before, and is increasing all the time.

Resources

This thriving population places ever greater demands on the Earth's **resources**, because of its need for **food**, **shelter**, and **fuel**. To accommodate these demands, people have changed the world around them to meet their needs.

- If all the land on Earth was shared equally among the entire population, we would all get an area equal in size to about 2.7 football pitches!

- The Earth is over 4 billion years old, but is only expected to support life for a further 500 million years.

- There are more than 1,000 artificial satellites and 21,000 pieces of man-made space debris currently orbiting the Earth!

- The length of a day on Earth is increasing by about 17 milliseconds per century!

Fun Facts

The force of gravity is not even all over the Earth. A person weighting 150 lbs at the equator would weight 151 lbs at the North Pole!

A green Earth makes a healthier environment.

Did You Know?

The part of Earth that has life on it is called the ecosphere.

49

PLANT LIFE ON EARTH

Plants!

Like all living things, plants rely on the gases in our **atmosphere** in order to survive, and it is thanks to them that we humans are able to breathe the air around us.

The very first **plant-like organisms** appeared in the Earth's oceans around 3,500 million years ago. They used light from the **Sun** to make food from **water** and **carbon dioxide**, releasing **oxygen** into the air as a by-product. This process is called **photosynthesis**, and was repeated over millions of years until there was enough oxygen in the atmosphere to support other forms of life.

Fun Facts

Some plants have evolved leaves, stings, or poisons to protect themselves from being eaten by animals!

Photosynthesis

The survival of almost all living things relies on the process of **photosynthesis**. Not only does it play an important role in maintaining the levels of **oxygen** and **carbon dioxide** in the **atmosphere**, it also keeps the plants we need for **food** health and ensures that they are able to **grow**, **reproduce**, and provide **habitats** - lush **rainforests** and shady **woodlands** - for a wide variety of **animal**, **bird**, and **insect** life.

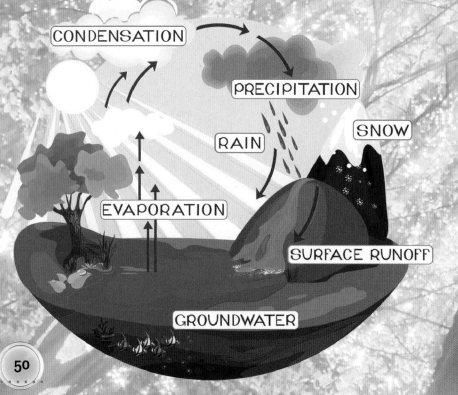

CONDENSATION

PRECIPITATION

SNOW

RAIN

EVAPORATION

SURFACE RUNOFF

GROUNDWATER

Adapting!

Like all living things, plants have had to adapt to their **environments** in order to survive. **Cacti** and many other **desert plants**, for example, store large quantities of water in their broad stems, and have **widespread root systems** that are able to collect water from a distance, because they grow in dry areas where there is very little rainfall.

- Everything we eat comes from plants, either directly, when we eat the plants ourselves, or indirectly, when the animals we eat feed on plants.
- All plants can be divided into two groups: **flowering plants**, including **roses, sunflowers**, and most types of **tree**, and **non-flowering plants**, such as **mosses** and **ferns**.
- Some plants eat insects, and other very tiny animals. They are called **carnivorous plants**, and grow in areas where the soil is thin, and lacking in nutrients.

Climates!

Arctic poppies, on the other hand, grow well in **cold climates**, on **mountains** and in **dry river beds**. They thrive amongst stones which absorb heat from the Sun, and provide shelter for their roots. Their flowers continually turn to face the Sun, tracking its progress across the sky.

Did You Know?

There are around 300,000 plant species living in the world today.

WATER WATER EVERYWHERE!

Around **71%** of the **Earth's surface is covered in water,** which makes up five huge **oceans**, and many smaller **seas**.

The world's oceans are not only very important to life on Earth, providing homes for vast numbers of living things, but also influence the **weather,** and **climate conditions** across the globe.

Ocean water is constantly moving in huge bands called **currents**.

The water absorbs **heat** from the **Sun**, particularly in **tropical regions**, and carries it all over the Earth in **surface currents**, which affect the top 350 metres of the ocean.

Fun Facts

Around 70% of the oxygen we breath is produced by the oceans!
The name 'Pacific Ocean' comes from the Latin "Tepre Pacificum" meaning "Peaceful Sea"

Very cold water from the **North and South Poles** sinks beneath the warmer surface currents and drifts towards the equator, where it is warmed by the Sun, and becomes a **surface current** itself. It then changes direction, drifting back towards the Poles, where it becomes a colder, **deep current** again.

Seas and oceans are constantly moved by **tides**, which are caused by the **Moon**.

As the Moon travels around the Earth, the force of its **gravity** makes the water on either side of the Earth bulge. In a 24 hour period, this causes two **high tides**, and two **low tides**, when sea levels are at their highest and lowest respectively.

Lake Superior is the largest of the Great Lakes of North America.

Did You Know ?

The Pacific is the largest of the world's oceans, and covers around 30% of the Earth's surface!

Rivers

Rivers form where **streams** join together, flowing across the land and eventually into a **sea** or **lake**.

Rivers alter the surface of the Earth over time by **eroding** the **rocks** they flow over, and by depositing **rocks, pebbles, sand,** and **silt** as they go.

At 6,853 km (4,258 miles) long, The Nile is the world's longest river!

SEA CREATURES!

The Earth's oceans are home to a startling array of plants and animals that live and feed at different levels of the water.

These levels are called **zones**.

The **sunlit zone** is home to all **ocean plants** and many animals from **corals** and **jellyfish**, to **seals, sea turtles**, and **sharks**. Billions of **microscopic plants** called **phytoplankton** drift near the surface of the water, and provide food for many of the creatures living within the ocean's depths.

Only a little light filters down to the **twilight zone**, so the animals that live here have adapted to life in near darkness, and are able to survive in very cold temperatures. These include **octopuses**, **squid**, **crabs**, and **lobsters**.

Fun Facts
A female octopus is called a "hen"! The Giant Pacific Octopus lays clutches of around 100,000 eggs!

The **sunless zone** is extremely cold, and the animals that live here feed mainly on dead **plankton**, which sinks from the surface of the water. This zone is extremely deep - it is difficult for humans to explore because the pressure of the water is so high. Animals that live here include **lantern fish, cookiecutter sharks**, and **deep sea jellyfish**.

The **abyssal zone** is freezing cold and completely dark. Many of the animals that live here, such as the **anglerfish** can produce light from their bodies to attract prey.

Did You Know ?

Most of an octopus's body is spongy and flexible, but its eyes are more solid. Most species of octopus can squeeze through tight spaces that are only slightly larger than their eyes! Bizarrely, an octopus's eyes remain at the same orientation regardless of its position, so if it turns on its side, or even flips upside down, its gaze will remain fixed!

- There are a million known species of plant and animal living in the world's oceans, and many more have yet to be discovered.

- Around 65,000 newly "discovered" species are still waiting to be given formal names.

- Coral reefs cover less than 1% of the ocean floor, but support around 25% of all marine creatures.

WEATHER CONDITIONS

What is Weather?

We use the word "**weather**" to describe the conditions in the **atmosphere** close to the Earth's surface. These conditions include **air temperature, wind speed, air pressure,** and the amount of water in the air, which we call **humidity**. Other factors include how **cloudy** it is, and whether there is any **precipitation (rain** or **snow)**.

The **Sun** plays a crucial part in determining the weather. Its rays have the strongest effect where they hit the surface of the Earth directly, around the planet's centre, or **equator**. The further away from the equator you are, the more the heat is spread over a larger area, so the weather is cooler.

Fun Facts

Regions along the equator receive the same strength of sunlight all year round. These places have only two distinguishable seasons: wet, and dry.

Different seasons

Weather conditions change throughout the year because the Earth is tilted on its **axis**. As the Earth **orbits** the Sun, the Sun's rays fall on different areas, causing the **seasons.**

The four major seasons are spring, summer, autumn, and winter.

Look how these trees respond to changes in the seasons.

Now it's sunny, now it's not...

Heat from the Sun causes water from the seas to **evaporate.** As the **water vapour** rises and cools, it **condenses**, forming tiny **water droplets** which group together to form **clouds**.

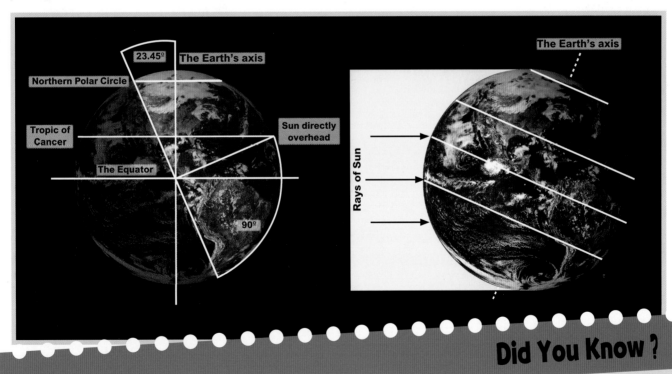

23.45°
The Earth's axis
Northern Polar Circle
Tropic of Cancer
Sun directly overhead
The Equator
90°
The Earth's axis
Rays of Sun

Did You Know?

When the North Pole of the Earth is tilted towards the Sun, we in the northern hemisphere get more sunlight: this is our summer. As the Earth travels around the Sun, the tilt of the North Pole changes. When it is tilted away from the Sun we receive less sunlight and it is winter. In between we have autumn and spring.

57

THE EARTH'S CLIMATE

Typical weather conditions and patterns in a region over time are known as its **climate**. Climates depend on the position of an area on the Earth's surface, and, accordingly, how much sunlight can reach it, as well as its **distance from the sea**, and its **height above sea level**.

Mountain climates drop as the **altitude** (height above sea level) increases, affecting the types of **vegetation** that are able to grow.

Polar climates are extremely cold and change very little throughout the year. There is hardly any rain or snowfall, and very few plants can grow. Polar animals have thick layers of fur or fat to keep them warm.

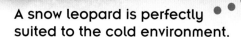

A snow leopard is perfectly suited to the cold environment.

Desert climates are very dry, and there is hardly any rainfall. Daytime temperatures are extremely warm, but can plummet over night. Many plants and animals that live in the desert can store water.

Mediterranean regions are warm all year round, but tend to be wet in **winter** and dry in **summer**. **Citrus fruits** grow well in Mediterranean climates because their thick skins prevent them from drying out in hot weather.

Areas around the **equator** are known as **equatorial regions**, and are permanently hot and wet; ideal conditions for **rainforests**.

City climates are usually warmer than the less built-up areas around them because concrete absorbs and retains heat for longer than vegetation.

In **temperate regions** the weather is changeable. Rain falls throughout the year, and temperatures vary according to the **season**.

Coastal or **maritime climates** are **mild** and **wet** because the air above the land and sea is constantly circulating, gaining and losing heat throughout the day and night.

The magnificent sea turtle.

Fun Facts

Tundra regions are known for their harsh winds and low winter temperatures. Only hardy, low-growing plants such a **lichens** are able to survive here.

Did You Know?

Tropical climates are warm all year round. There are only two seasons: the dry season, and the wet season.

HABITATS

Tigers have **striped fur** to help them hide amongst the long grasses and blend in with the sunlight filtering through the treetops to the jungle floor. With their **stealthy hunting methods**, huge paws, **sharp claws** and **fearsome** jaws, tigers are **formidable predators** and are well adapted to thrive in the **grasslands** and **forests** in which they live.

Frogs are highly adapted animals.

The tiger is the biggest cat in the world.

Tree frogs eat insects and other small animals. Many can **change colour** to blend in with their surroundings and surprise their prey. They have **sticky pads** on their feet to stop them falling.

Fun Facts

In order to thrive in their natural surroundings, plants and animals have had to adapt to the world around them.

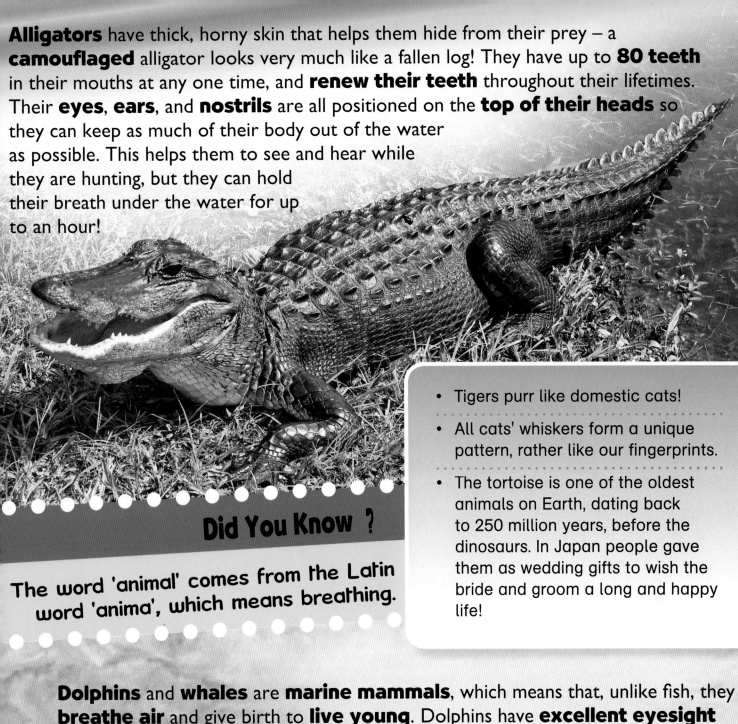

Alligators have thick, horny skin that helps them hide from their prey – a **camouflaged** alligator looks very much like a fallen log! They have up to **80 teeth** in their mouths at any one time, and **renew their teeth** throughout their lifetimes. Their **eyes**, **ears**, and **nostrils** are all positioned on the **top of their heads** so they can keep as much of their body out of the water as possible. This helps them to see and hear while they are hunting, but they can hold their breath under the water for up to an hour!

Did You Know ?

The word 'animal' comes from the Latin word 'anima', which means breathing.

- Tigers purr like domestic cats!

- All cats' whiskers form a unique pattern, rather like our fingerprints.

- The tortoise is one of the oldest animals on Earth, dating back to 250 million years, before the dinosaurs. In Japan people gave them as wedding gifts to wish the bride and groom a long and happy life!

Dolphins and **whales** are **marine mammals**, which means that, unlike fish, they **breathe air** and give birth to **live young**. Dolphins have **excellent eyesight** and **hearing**, and can **communicate** with each other by making **clicking** and **whistling sounds**. They make particularly **high-pitched clicking sounds** to help them **navigate** and find food. This process is known as **echolocation.**

OPEN TO CHANGE

In order to thrive in their natural surroundings, plants and animals have had to **adapt** to the world around them.

Kangaroos, for example, are ideally suited to life in the **harsh climate** of the **Australian outback** because they are able to survive for long periods without water. When they do need to look for food and water, they can reach speeds of up to **70 kilometres an hour**, and their **energy-efficient** way of travelling means that they can cover long distances in no time!

Fun Facts

The red kangaroo is the world's largest marsupial. Females have one baby at a time, which at birth is smaller than a cherry!.

Tropical pitchers are carnivorous plants that lure prey into their traps with their **sweet smell** and **sugary nectar**. As well as unsuspecting insects, larger species of pitcher plant are able to attract and digest larger animals, including mice and lizards.

Most species are found in **southeast Asia**. It is believed that monkeys drink rainwater out of the pitcher-shaped plants, giving them their alternative name: **"monkey cups"**!

Unlike other species of bear, **polar bears** have adapted to be able to thrive in water and on land. They are **excellent swimmers**, and have been spotted over 100 miles away from land or ice.

They have large, **furry-soled feet** which not only help them to spread their weight on snow and ice, but also keep them warm and stop them slipping. As well as providing **insulation**, their **white fur** provides a **camouflage**, and their **small ears prevent heat loss** in the freezing Arctic climate.

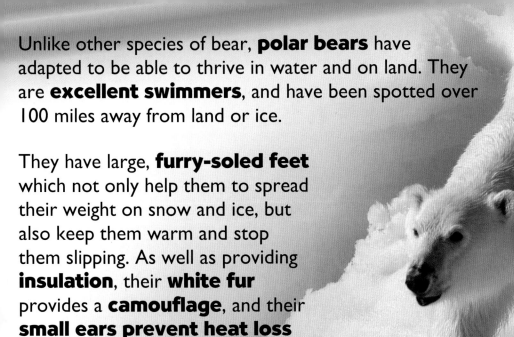

They may not be pretty, but vultures are nature's cleaning agents!

Polar bears are found in the Arctic, the lands around the North Pole, where it is near impossible for human beings to survive.

Vultures are scavengers. They glide on air currents, searching the ground below for carcasses to feed upon. Their bald heads and necks help them to stay clean by preventing bacteria from animal remains from festering in their feathers and spreading disease.

Did You Know ?

Polar bears actually have black skins and colourless fur! Their thick, hollow hairs reflect light, giving the bears their white-looking coats.

NATURAL RESOURCES

As we have already learned, the world's growing **population** is placing ever greater demands on the planet's **resources**. Many of these resources are beneath the Earth's surface. These include **precious stones**, **metals**, and **fuels.**

Fossil Fuels

Coal, **oil**, and **gas** are known as **fossil fuels**. They have many uses, including running motor vehicles and generating **electricity**.

Fossil fuels are formed from the remains of plants and animals that have been buried in rock for millions of years. The **chemical energy** trapped in these **organisms** is released as they are burned.

Because demand for these fuels is so great, and they take such a long time to form, supplies are limited.

Nuclear Power

Radioactive substances produce **nuclear energy** when their **atoms** are broken apart. Many people believe that **nuclear power** could be the most efficient, and convenient, energy source of the future, but it creates hazardous **radioactive waste**, which is difficult to dispose of safely.

Mining

Mining and **extracting fuels** and **ores** from beneath the surface of the Earth is a difficult – and expensive – process, made harder by the fact that many sources have already been used up.

Re-using and **recycling** materials help to make the Earth's **natural resources** last longer, but scientists are having to look for other sources of fuel to meet the population's growing needs.

Coal, one of nature's most valuable natural resources, is created from dead plant matter!

Renewable Energy!

Only 5% of the Earth's energy comes from **renewable sources**, that is, sources of energy that will not run out. These include heat from the Sun (**solar energy**), and from underground rocks (**geothermal energy**), as well as wind, which can be used to turn **wind turbines**, and moving water, which is used in **hydroelectric power stations.**

Renewable energy is often less reliable and efficient than fossil fuels because it relies on certain weather conditions in order to be effective.

Fun Facts

The largest wind turbines generate enough electricity to supply around 600 homes!

Did You Know?

Coal has the largest remaining reserves of all the fossil fuels, but as the growing population continues to use more and more, demand is soon likely to outstrip supply. It is thought that we currently have enough coal to meet around 180 years of global production.

My First DICTIONARY

Words · Meanings

Plants · Animals

Objects · Examples

A fun reference book of first words

A

above
up or higher

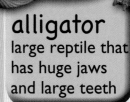

alligator
large reptile that has huge jaws and large teeth

art
art can be anything, including a painting, sculpture, drawing, music, photograph, or any other form of expression

astronaut
person whose job is to explore space

awake
state of not being asleep

award
something you get for doing well

awash
state of being covered with water

academy
institution for the advancement of knowledge

act
to do something or perform a role

addition
adding of numbers to get a sum

address
an address states where someone lives or works

aeroplane
flying vehicle with fixed wings and an engine

adjective
word that describes a place, thing or person

adult
grown up man or woman

adverb
an adverb states 'how', 'when', 'where', or 'how much'. Examples include *quickly, easily, mainly,* etc.

afraid
state of being frightened or scared

alike
when two or more objects are similar, they're alike

anatomy
science of the body

ant
small, social insects

ambulance
vehicle that takes sick or injured people to the hospital

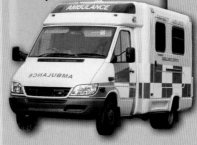

ape
large tailless primate

arm
part of the human body between the shoulder and the elbow

arrows
long, thin objects with a sharp point

axe
sharp metal tool used to chop wood

B

batter
uncooked, liquid mixture of eggs, flour, butter and other ingredients. Cakes, cookies and muffins are made from batter

baboon
large monkey with large cheek pouches and a big snout

baby
very young child

banana
sweet, yellow fruit

barn
farm building where animals and their food are kept

bagel
bread roll shaped like a doughnut

beads
small objects with a hole through them. Used to make jewellery

book
composition of words that has been published

bear
big, furry animal

brush
object used to clean, paint or groom

bulb
turns electricity into light

burrow
tunnel or hole dug by a small animal

blast
sudden and very loud noise

brain
organ that helps us to think. The brain is protected by the skull

brave
someone who is not afraid to face dangerous situations

broken
state of something that has been separated into two or more pieces

broom
object used to sweep the floor

bus
large road vehicle that transports people

cab
another name for a taxi

cabbage
leafy plant eaten as a vegetable

cake
sweet dessert

can
container that stores food and drink

candle
stick made of wax that has a wick

cap
type of hat

cast
throw forcefully

chair
piece of furniture that people can sit on

cabin
simple house usually made of wood

camel
large mammal that lives in desert areas

chart
diagram that shows the relationship between things

chimney
structure that funnels smoke away from a fire

chisel
tool with flat blade and sharp edge

circle
round figure where all points are an equal distance from the centre

cliff
steep structure of soil and rock

cone
shape that has a point at one end and a circular opening at the other

cry
to shed tears from the eyes

courage
quality to face danger or pain without showing too much fear

crawl
moving with body near the ground

C

cub
the young of certain animals, such as lions and bears

cube
geometric figure with six square sides

curtains
material hung to provide a covering or screen

couple
two similar objects in a pair or two people

crane
long-necked bird that lives in wet areas

n o p q r s t u v w x y z

D

dirty
opposite of clean

dad
another word for father

dark
opposite of light

deer
long-legged mammals that have hooved feet

daughter
female child

December
last month of the year

desert
very dry area

diamond
very hard, shiny jewel

dog
pet animals commonly kept by humans

dollar
currency used in many countries

doll
a small figure kept as a toy

dolphin
marine mammal with teeth and a long nose

door
entrance to a house or room

down
opposite of up

drain
a channel or pipe that carries liquid away

dress
piece of clothing with a top and a skirt

drill
to make a hole

drop
to let something fall

doctor
person who says what's wrong with you when you're ill

duck
bird that swims well and lives near the water

dusk
time of day after sunset

drum
musical instrument

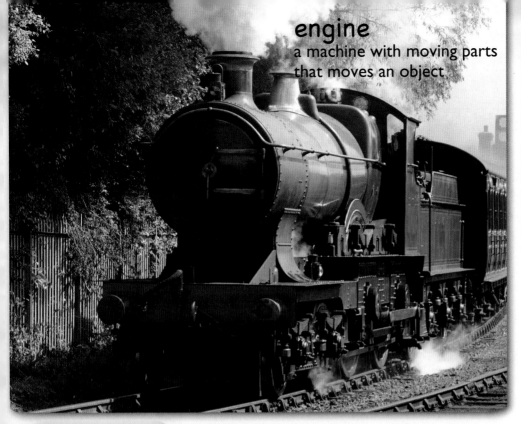

engine
a machine with moving parts that moves an object

E

Europe
continent in the Northern Hemisphere, including the UK, Ireland, Italy, Germany, France and Spain

excellent
very good; outstanding

eagle
large bird of prey with a hooked beak and sharp talons

egg
an oval or round object laid by most non-mammal female creatures

elbow
joint in the middle of the arm

eleven
ten plus one

emperor
ruler of a country

empty
containing nothing

entrance
an opening

envelope
folded paper or card to contain letters and other items

eraser
object used to rub off pencil marks

eager
having or showing keen interest or desire

earn
to receive something for working

elephant
largest land animal, with a long trunk

exercise
physical or mental exertion that is done to improve health and performance

extinct
to have died-out as a species. Extinct animals include dodos and dinosaurs

n o p q r s t u v w x y z

F

fast
ability to act or move quickly

fawn
young deer

fear
to be afraid or scared

femur
upper leg bone, which is the longest in the human body

fin
fish have fins that help them swim

flag
square or rectangular piece of material that represents a country, state, province, or city

flower
the part of the plant containing the organs that make new plants, usually surrounded by petals

face
front of the head carrying features such as the mouth and nose

factory
a building where things are made or put together

falcon
bird of prey that hunts other birds and small animals

family
group of people who are related to each other

famous
very well known

farmer
person who looks after animals and produces food by growing plants

firefighter
person who puts out fires and saves lives

fork
object with prongs used for eating solid food

fraction
part of a whole. Half of an orange is a fraction of an orange

foal
young horse

funnel
conical shaped structure with a wide opening at one end and a narrow opening at the other

furniture
tables, beds and chairs are all furniture

furrow
a long narrow trench in the ground for planting seeds or helping water drain

fruit
part of some plants that contain seeds. Apples and oranges are fruits

future
time that is yet to come

G

gibe
make fun of

giddy
condition of having a dizzying sensation

give
when you let someone have something, you 'give' the person that thing

glasses
objects used to help people see more clearly

glue
substance that sticks things together

gibbon
small, tree-dwelling ape found in Asia

gnat
small flying insect

gold
precious metal. Some coins and jewellery are made of gold

golf
sport where a ball is hit into a series of holes using metal sticks called clubs

grandparents
the mother and father of each of your parents

gift
something you give someone without asking anything in return

grass
common plant that forms a green covering over the ground

grate
to make into very small shreds

guest
visitor to a house

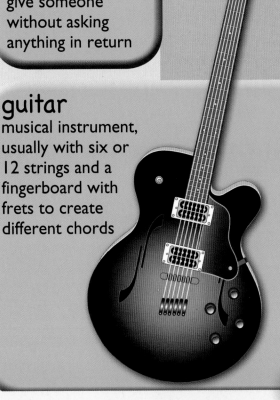

guitar
musical instrument, usually with six or 12 strings and a fingerboard with frets to create different chords

garden
man-made area where plants and flowers grow

gate
a hinged barrier in a fence

gather
to collect

gazelle
a small slender antelope found in Africa and Asia

geography
study of the location of people and features on earth

geyser
natural hot spring that sprays steam and water above the ground

H

haystack
big pile of hay

habitat
natural place where animals and plants live

hail
pellets of frozen rain that fall from clouds

ham
meat from a pig's leg that is salted and dried or smoked

harp
musical instrument with many strings

hat
a shaped covering, worn on the head

hatchet
axe with a short handle

heart
an organ made of muscle that pumps blood around the body

hem
a sewn edge of a piece of material

herbivore
plant-eating animal

hero
person with courage and character who is known for their good deeds

hoe
garden tool with a long handle and flat blade

hoof
hard, protective covering on the feet of some animals. Deer, zebras and horses have hooves

hornet
wasp-like flying insect capable of stinging

honey
a sweet, sticky liquid made by bees from nectar

hound
a dog bred to track animals by scent

hurricane
dangerous storm with fast winds and heavy rainfall

hyena
meat-eating animal that hunts and scavenges prey

hamster
small rodent sometimes kept as a pet

hose
flexible pipe through which water flows, usually used to water plants

a b c d e f g (h) (i) (j) k l m

I

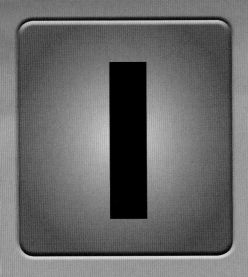

iceberg
a large floating mass of ice that has separated from an ice sheet

icicle
hanging ice that forms when dripping water freezes over time

igloo
house made from blocks of ice

impala
a graceful antelope found in large herds in southern Africa

infant
a very young child or baby

irate
feeling or showing great anger

island
piece of land surrounded by water

J

jacket
short coat

janitor
someone who cleans a building

K

jab
poke abruptly

jet
fast and
powerful aeroplane

jewel
precious stone

judo
a form of martial arts

junk
traditional Chinese
sailing ship build
from wood

justice
when something
is treated fairly
and reasonably

kangaroo
a large marsupial
with powerful
back legs found
in Australia

kayak
small, narrow boat

kennel
shelter for dogs

kidney
bean-shaped organs
in the human
body that helps to
produce urine

kilt
traditional dress
worn by the people
of Scotland

kiwi
flightless bird found
in New Zealand

knee
part of the
body where
the leg bends

label
paper or fabric attached to an item that gives information

lace
delicate fabric

ladle
large spoon used to serve gravy and soup

lake
large body of water surrounded by land

lane
narrow road in a rural area

lemonade
drink made from lemons, water and sugar

laundry
clothing that is about to be washed or has just been washed

lava
molten rock that erupts from volcanoes

lawn
an area covered with short grass that is maintained

lever
a rigid bar attached to a pivot, used to help move things

library
a building or room containing books and other material that you can use and borrow

lifeboat
a small boat used to evacuate a larger ship; a boat launched from land to save people in trouble at sea

link
a relationship between two things

log
short piece of a tree trunk or branch

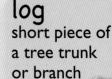

liquid
one of the three forms of matter, with gasses and solids being the others. Water is a liquid

lobster
a large marine crustacean with claws

lunch
meal eaten in the middle of the day

lungs
organs through which animals breathe

L

lamb
baby sheep

M

macaroni
narrow tubes
of pasta

magician
An artist who
performs magic is
known as a magician.
Magic is the art of
performing illusions
and tricks

magnifying glass
lens that can make
things look bigger
than their actual size

mailbox
box where
letters are put

mammal
typically any warm-
blooded animal with
hair or fur. Mammals
nourish their young
with milk

mammoth
large, elephant-like
animal of the Ice Ages

marsh
wet and grassy land

marsupial
mammals with pouches,
where the young are
kept. Kangaroos and
koalas are marsupials

meal
good amount of food
eaten at one time

medal
award given for a
good performance

metal
shiny, solid element
that can conduct heat
and electricity. Gold,
copper, silver and iron
are metals

mountain
natural elevation from the earth's surface that is higher than a hill

mittens
thick gloves that keep the hands warm

mole
burrowing mammal with powerful claws and poor eyesight

mosaic
work of art made up of pieces of glass, tiles, stones, or other objects fitted together

moth
nocturnal flying insect related to butterflies

muffin
small cake

mummy
preserved dead body usually related to Ancient Egypt

museum
a building where objects of interest are displayed

n o p q r s t u v w x y z

N

nail
hard surface that grows at the end of the fingers and toes

nag
bother or worry persistently

nanny
person employed to care for a child in their own home

napkin
something with which you clean your face after eating

narrow
not very wide, usually in relation to an object's length or height

nap
short sleep during the day

nest
structure made of twigs where birds lay eggs and take care of their young

neat
clean and proper

neighbour
someone living close to your house

neon
gas that is used in some lights

new
condition of something that has never been used before

newspaper
printed publication that gives information about current events of public interest

newt
bright-coloured amphibian

nib
the pointed end part of a pen

nightingale
bird that is known for singing beautiful songs

nocturnal
condition of being more active at night than the daytime. Bats are nocturnal creatures

nod
the up and down movement of the head

note
short written message

noun
word that represents a person, place or thing

nut
fruit with a hard shell

nurse
person that looks after you when you are sick

noodles
strips of pasta or similar dough, typically made with eggs

nutmeg
seed of a tropical tree that is used as a spice

a b c d e f g h i j k l m

oar
tool generally made of wood that is used to row a boat

observatory
place from where people observe the skies, using tools such as telescopes

ocean
a very large expanse of sea

oil
a thick, sticky liquid made from petrol

Olympics
the Olympic games began in ancient Greece over 2,700 years ago. The games are held every four years

octopus
creature that has eight arms covered in suction cups

olive
small oval fruit

omnivore
animal that eats both plants and meat. Humans are omnivores

omit
to leave out

orbit
fixed path that one object takes to circle around another. The moon orbits the earth, and the earth orbits the sun

orca
a large toothed member of the dolphin family with black and white markings

ostrich
largest bird in the world

otter
playful aquatic mammal

ounce
unit of weight that is one-twelfth of a pound

oval
rounded egg shape

oven
an enclosed compartment used for cooking food

ox
another name for a cow or bull

orchid
colourful flower that grows in warm areas

oyster
soft-bodied mollusk with a hard protective shell often eaten raw as a delicacy

ozone
colourless toxic gas that forms a protective layer from the sun in our atmosphere

overcoat
long warm coat worn over clothing

P

pebble
small, smooth stone

package
object or objects, placed in a box or wrapped for transport

paddle
a short oar used for rowing a small boat

pail
container with a handle

palette
thin board, on which an artist mixes paint

party
social gathering of invited guests

pentagon
five-sided shape

pepper
spice people use on their food

pod
group of whales

pupil
person who is learning in an educational institution

proverb
short saying that is a commonly known truth

puppet
small doll that is made to move by pulling strings

puzzle
game that requires logic and knowledge to solve it

Q

qualm
feeling of doubt and uneasiness

quack
the sound of a duck

quarter
the portion of something when divided equally into four; coin worth 25 American cents

quicksand
loose, wet sand where objects can sink

quiet
calm or without noise

quilt
a warm bed covering made of padding between layers of fabric stitched together

quip
to make a joke or a witty remark

quit
give up; go away or leave

quiver
container where arrows are kept

quiz
a test of knowledge

R

rake
garden tool that helps to collect leaves and grass

rabbit
small mammal with big ears

racket
loud and disturbing noise

radar
device that is used to locate objects at a distance

radio
communication device where you can listen to music and talk shows

radius
distance from the centre of a circle to the border

raisin
dried grape

rattle
series of short, rapid knocking sounds

recipe
set of instructions for making a particular dish, usually of food

a b c d e f g h i j k l m

reef
a ridge of jagged rock, coral or sand just above or below the surface of the sea

refrigerator
machine that keeps food cold and fresh

rein
strap that a rider controls and steers a horse with

rhinoceros
large, thick-skinned animal with one or two horns on its head

rhyme
to have similar sounds, like 'kite' and 'light', 'bite' and 'right' etc.

robot
machine programmed to move automatically and perform specific functions

rocket
a tube filled with fuel that can be propelled to great heights

rodent
mammal whose two front teeth grow constantly. Mice, squirrels, hamsters, and rats are all rodents

roof
covering of a room or building

roost
to sit on a perch

rooster
male chicken

roots
plant parts below the ground that get water and other nutrients from the soil

route
the way or course taken to get to a destination

rug
floor covering made of thick fabric

S

scroll
a roll of parchment or paper for writing or painting on

shrub
low-lying bush with a woody stem

silk
delicate thread used to make fine fabric

sack
container made of fabric, paper or plastic that you can put things in

sill
wood that forms the base of a window

sail
large piece of strong fabric that catches wind and helps a boat move through the water

seal
a device or substance that joins two items together

silo
a tower or pit used to store grain

scallop
an edible mollusk with a ribbed, fan-shaped shell

season
each of winter, spring, summer, and autumn that mark particular weather patterns and daylight hours

skull
bony structure of the head that protects the brain

sleet
freezing rain

shovel
tool used to dig and move material

slither
to move smoothly and without obstruction

snail
a mollusk with a spiral shell that the whole body can be withdrawn into

steak
slice of meat or fish for grilling or frying

swap
to give something in exchange for something else

synthesizer
musical instrument that electronically creates sounds

strait
narrow body of water connecting two bigger bodies of water

snap
to break something in two, usually with a cracking sound

soil
the upper layer of earth in which plants grow

swamp
wet area that usually has a lot of animal and plant life

sphere
ball-shaped object

T

tablet
a flat slab of stone, clay or wood

tambourine
shallow drum with metal discs used as a percussion instrument

toddler
a young child just beginning to walk

telescope
instrument through which distant objects appear closer

tent
shelter made of fabric that can be moved

tie
narrow band of fabric that is tied around the neck

thunder
a loud rumbling or crashing sound heard after lightning due to rapidly expanding air

tongs
simple pincer tool used to pick things up

tornado
rapidly spinning air that is shaped like a funnel

town
urban area smaller than a city

tract
large area of land

a b c d e f g h i j k l m

tractor
powerful farm vehicle, usually with large treaded wheels

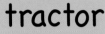

truce
state of peace between two opposing parties

trust
to be confident about and have faith in something

tub
large vessel for holding or storing liquids

tuck
to push, fold or turn something to hold it in place

trail
rough path

triangle
a shape with three straight sides

trunk
tree's major support

tugboat
sturdy boat that guides other bigger boats in and out of harbours

twister
another name for a tornado – rapidly spinning air that can be very dangerous

trout
a fish of the salmon family often fished for food

U

ukulele
small four-stringed guitar with its origins in Hawaii

unicorn
mythical, one-horned animal

uniform
special outfit worn by members of one particular group

unite
combine or join

urban
located in or related to a city

urge
very strong desire

V

vase
a decorative container used for displaying flowers

utensils
tools used in the kitchen, like forks, knives and spoons

W

vat
large tub that is used to holds liquids

veteran
a person who has long experience in a particular field

vine
plant that does not have a support of its own and grows on other objects

vocabulary
group of words that a person knows and understands

vote
a formal choice someone gives between candidates or options

vowel
any of the letters a, e, i, o, and u

wagon
vehicle with wheels that is drawn by a tractor or animals

wand
thin rod that magicians carry

watch
small clock that you normally wear on the wrist

weary
state of being very tired

weasel
small, furry mammals having short legs

whisk
tool used to beat eggs or batter

wrench
tool that is used to turn nuts or bolts

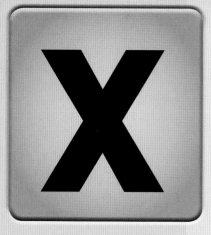

X

yam
the American name for the sweet potato, a vegetable

yard
small area of land attached to a house

yelp
bark in a high-pitched tone

yore
something of a long time ago

Z

x-ray
special picture of your teeth or bones taken in a hospital or a dentists

yardstick
a measuring stick equal to one yard, or three feet, in length

xylophone
musical instrument with rows of bars

yarn
cord of twisted fibre that is used in weaving and sewing

yacht
a medium-sized boat with sails

Y

yell
to shout in a loud voice

zebra
horse-like animal with black and white stripes

zigzag
line or course with abrupt left and right turns

zeal
great energy or enthusiasm in pursuit of a cause or objective

zip
two strips of metal or plastic that are joined together with a slider

yak
large wild ox with shaggy hair, humped shoulders and large horns

yolk
yellow portion of an egg

zero
no quantity or number; naught

zoologist
scientist who studies animals

My First ATLAS

Minerals

Monuments

Places

Resources

Maps

People

A visual guide to the countries of the world

CANADA AND THE USA

Canada is geographically bigger than the United States, but the latter is nine times more populated.

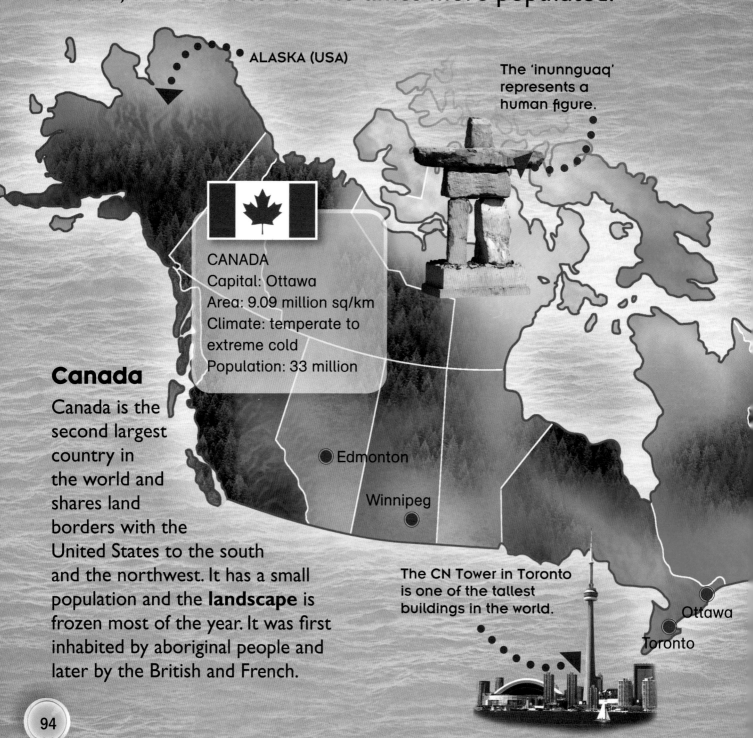

ALASKA (USA)

The 'inunnguaq' represents a human figure.

CANADA
Capital: Ottawa
Area: 9.09 million sq/km
Climate: temperate to extreme cold
Population: 33 million

Canada

Canada is the second largest country in the world and shares land borders with the United States to the south and the northwest. It has a small population and the **landscape** is frozen most of the year. It was first inhabited by aboriginal people and later by the British and French.

Edmonton

Winnipeg

The CN Tower in Toronto is one of the tallest buildings in the world.

Ottawa

Toronto

United States of America

The United States of America is a huge country with 50 states. The country is situated mostly in central North America, with Washington, D.C. as its capital. The United States lies between the Pacific and Atlantic Oceans, bordered by Canada to the north and Mexico to the south. The country is regarded as the most powerful nation in the world with lots of **natural resources.**

The Statue of Liberty in New York was gifted to the US by France.

Seattle

United States of America
Capital: Washington, D.C.
Area: 9.16 million sq/km
Climate: mostly temperate
Population: 307 million

Denver

Los Angeles

Chicago

Washington, D.C.

Dallas

Alaska

Alaska is the country's biggest state, but also the least dense in terms of population. It once belonged to Russia, before the US purchased it in 1867 for $7.2 million!

Fun Facts

The venus fly trap only lives in the wild in the Carolinas and nowhere else in the world.

DID YOU KNOW?

Basketball was invented by a Canadian named Dr. James Naismith. He invented the game while working in Boston with college students.

MEXICO AND CENTRAL AMERICA

Mexico and Central America form a natural bridge linking the United States with South America. The culturally rich region is full of ancient, historical ruins.

Mexico

Mexico is famous for its culture, especially the largely untouched ruins of the Mayan civilisation. This country of over 100 million is full of natural splendour — from the lovely plains and mountains to its beautiful coastline.

MEXICO
Capital: Mexico City
Area: 1.92 million sq/km
Climate: tropical to desert
Population: 111 million

Fun Facts

Mexico City hosted the nineteenth Olympic Games in 1968. It is the only Latin America country to do so. It has also hosted the FIFA World Cup twice, in 1970 and 1986.

Nicaragua

Nicaragua is the largest Central American country. Its history is tainted by civil wars, and volcanoes and earthquakes are always a threat to this country. However, it has its share of natural attractions. The coral reefs and the mangrove forests are rich with flora and fauna, and are a big hit with tourists.

Chichen Itza in Mexico — remains of the mighty Maya civilisation.

Mexico City

Guatemala City

Belmopan

Managua

Costa Rica

Costa Rica is located between the Pacific Ocean and the Caribbean Sea. Its picturesque landscape makes this small country an ideal tourist destination. Costa Rica literally translates as 'rich coast' and the country is known for its coffee production.

Since 1828, the Poas volcano in Costa Rica has erupted 39 times.

Belize

Belize is located on the Caribbean coast of Central America. The landscape is sprinkled with Maya ruins and **diverse** animal life, ranging from the jaguar to the toucan monkey. Belize also has the Western Hemisphere's longest coral reef.

BELIZE
Capital: Belmopan
Area: 22,806 sq/km
Climate: tropical
Population: 307,000

COSTA RICA
Capital: San Jose
Area: 50,660 sq/km
Climate: tropical and subtropical
Population: 4.2 million

San Jose

NORTH ANDEAN COUNTRIES

North Andean countries include Ecuador, Bolivia, Peru and Colombia.

Colombia

Colombia is the only country to touch both the Atlantic and the Pacific oceans. Colombia is famous for its jewellery, especially its emeralds. It is also known for having the continent's highest coal production. The climate is tropical because of its proximity to the equator, but there are peaks that are covered in snow owing to the altitude.

Ecuador

Ecuador is located on the northwestern corner of the South American continent. It has Colombia to its north, and Peru to the southeast. The Galapagos Islands are a part of Ecuador, and the country has some of the greatest **biodiversity** of any country in the world. The climate is mostly tropical, with an extreme rainy season.

ECUADOR
Capital: Quito
Area: 276,840 sq/km
Climate: mostly tropical
Population: 14.5 million

COLOMBIA
Capital: Bogota
Area: 1.03 million sq/km
Climate: tropical to cool
Population: 45 million

The Andes

The Andes mountain range dominates the west of the South American continent and is one of the longest mountain ranges in the world. It is over 7,000 km (4,400 miles) long, and 700 km (300 miles) at its widest. The average height of its mountains is about 4000 m (13,000 ft).

Fun Facts

The Galapagos volcanoes, 960 km (597 miles) west of Ecuador, bring a lot of tourists to the country because of their unique and diverse flora and fauna.

PERU
Capital: Lima
Area: 1.28 million sq/km
Climate: diverse (tropical to cool)
Population: 29 million

Peru

Peru is the largest country in South America after Brazil and Argentina. It is unique for having three different landscapes – the rocky Andes, the Atacama Desert, and the Amazonian forest.

A colourful market in Otavalo, Ecuador.

The Machu Picchu ruins - remnants of a once-powerful Incc Empire.

Bogota

Quito

Lima

BRAZIL AND NEIGHBOURING COUNTRIES

Brazil is South America's biggest country. Its neighbours include Argentina, Peru, Paraguay, Colombia, Venezuela, Suriname, Guyana, and Bolivia.

Guyana

Originally a Dutch colony in the 17th century, by 1815 Guyana had come under British rule. It is also one of the four non-Spanish-speaking territories on the continent, along with the states of Brazil (Portuguese) and Suriname (Dutch), and the French overseas region of French Guiana (French).

Trinidad and Tobago

The islands of Trinidad and Tobago may be close to each other, but have their own distinctive cultural flavours. Trinidad, mainly inhabited by people of African and Indian descent, is known for its steel music. Tobago, the smaller of the two islands, is slower paced and more scenic.

The Itaipu dam is the world's most powerful electricity generating station.

TRINIDAD AND TOBAGO
Capital: Port of Spain
Area: 5,128 sq km
Climate: tropical
Population: 1.2 million

VENEZUELA
Capital: Caracas
Area: 882,050 sq/km
Climate: tropical and moderate
Population: 27 million

GUYANA
Capital: Georgetown
Area: 196,850 sq/km
Climate: tropical
Population: 772,000

BRAZIL
Capital: Brasilia
Area: 8.45 million sq/km
Climate: mostly tropical
Population: 199 million

Caracas
Port of Spain
Georgetown
Paramaribo
Cayenne

Brasilia

Suriname

Suriname is home to the Maroons – descendants of African slaves who arrived about 300 years back. Its capital is Paramaribo.

Brazil

Brazil is the largest country in the continent occupying nearly half of South America. Brazil is also the fifth most populated country and the fourth most populated democracy in the world. Football is the national sport and is followed religiously.

The Statue of Christ, Rio de Janeiro, Brazil.

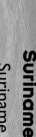

Fun Facts

The Statue of Christ, the 130 ft tall statue that overlooks Rio de Janeiro, is one of the seven wonders of modern times. This sculpture is the symbol and icon of Brazil.

ARGENTINA AND NEIGHBOURING COUNTRIES

Argentina borders Paraguay and Bolivia to the north, Brazil and Uruguay to the northeast, and Chile to the west and south.

Argentina

Argentina is the second largest country in South America and eighth in the world. The country's culture is heavily shaped by the Europeans, most particularly the Italians and Spanish people, who formed the largest percentage of newcomers from 1860 to 1930.

The Atacama Desert dominates the Chilean landscape.

La Paz, Bolivia, is the highest capital city in the world.

La Paz

Asuncion

Montevideo

Buenos Aires

Santiago

Argentina is the birthplace of the graceful dance, tango.

PARAGUAY
Capital: Asuncion
Area: 397,300 sq/km
Climate: subtropical to temperate
Population: 7 million

URUGUAY
Capital: Montevideo
Area: 173,620 sq/km
Climate: warm, temperate
Population: 3.5 million

Uruguay

Uruguay is located in the southeastern part of the continent and is typified by low grasslands. It has the highest literacy rate and the lowest poverty rate in the continent and education is compulsory and free. The economy of the country is dominated by agriculture.

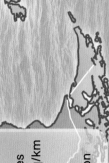

ARGENTINA
Capital: Buenos Aires
Area: 2.73 million sq/km
Climate: mostly temperate
Population: 41 million

CHILE
Capital: Santiago
Area: 748,800 sq/km
Climate: Diverse (temperate to cool and dry)
Population: 16.5 million

Chile

Chile is 4,000 km (2,485 miles) long and only 150 km (93 miles) wide on average. Eighty per cent of the country is covered by mountains. People are mostly of European descent or a mixture of European and indigenous ancestry. In the Atacama desert lie the Chuquicamata and Escondida copper mines.

Fun Facts

Argentina's population is predominantly of European descent after a wave of European investment and immigration around 1870.

WESTERN EUROPE

Western Europe generally refers to the countries in the westernmost half of Europe, although exact definitions vary.

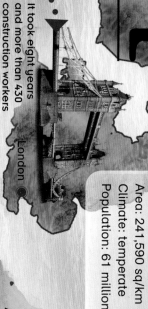

It took eight years and more than 430 construction workers to build Tower Bridge, London.

SPAIN
Capital: Madrid
Area: 499,542 sq/km
Climate: temperate
Population: 41 million

Lisbon

Madrid

Bullfighting is still passionately followed in Spain

FRANCE
Capital: Paris
Area: 545,630 sq/km
Climate: cool winters and mild summers
Population: 64 million

The Eiffel Tower, Paris, is the tallest building in France and one of the world's most famous structures.

Paris

London

The United Kingdom
The North Sea and the English Channel separate the United Kingdom from the rest of Europe. The countries of England, Scotland, Wales, and Northern Ireland make up the United Kingdom. England is the region's most populous area with 49 million inhabitants.

UNITED KINGDOM
Capital: London
Area: 241,590 sq/km
Climate: temperate
Population: 61 million

Amsterdam

GERMANY
Capital: Berlin
Area: 349,223 sq/km
Climate: temperate
Population: 82 million

Rome

Berlin

Prague

Vienna

Ljubljana

Alpine countries
Alpine states refer to the countries associated with the Alps region. As defined by the Alpine Convention of 1991, the region of the Alps comprises of the territories of seven countries. These seven states of the Alps are Switzerland, Liechtenstein, Austria, Slovenia, Germany, France and Italy.

Spain
Spain dominates most of the Iberian Peninsula in southwest Europe. The landscape is dominated by high plateaus with mountain ranges. The nation was a dominant force in Europe during the 16th and 17th centuries. Bull fighting remains a major attraction, despite increasing opposition to its cruelty.

Fun Facts
Belgium is nicknamed 'the battlefield of Europe' and 'the cockpit of Europe' due to its strategic role in the World Wars.

NORTHERN EUROPE

Northern Europe is a loose term that generally includes the Nordic countries of northernmost Europe, including: Sweden, Finland, Iceland, Denmark and Norway.

Sweden

Sweden is a highly successful and peaceful northern European country with high levels of literacy and employment. It is the third biggest country in the European Union by landmass, with about 85 percent of the people residing in urban areas. The landscape is mostly low and flat.

Norway

Norway is partitioned by mountains and has a fjord-rich shoreline that is over 21,000 km (13,050 miles) long. Its merchant and oil fleets are among the world's largest. This country of over 4.6 million boasts an extremely high literacy rate.

NORWAY
Capital: Oslo
Area: 307,442 sq/km
Climate: temperate to cool
Population: 4.6 million

Finland

Finland, in northern Europe, has a mountainous landscape in the north and is low-lying in the centre and the south. The population is mostly concentrated in the triangle formed by the cities of Tampere, Turku, and Helsinki. The country is home to over 180,000 lakes well complemented by rich coniferous forests.

FINLAND
Capital: Helsinki
Area: 304,473 sq/km
Climate: cold to temperate
Population: 5.2 million

The whooper swan is the national bird of Finland.

This Sami Teepee is the Norwegian version of the Native American tent.

SWEDEN
Capital: Stockholm
Area: 410,934 sq/km
Climate: diverse (temperate to cold)
Population: 9 million

Helsinki

Stockholm

Oslo

Fun Facts

Denmark once controlled the whole of northern Europe and was a very important power. It is where the play *Hamlet* by William Shakespeare is set.

DID YOU KNOW?

Sweden is connected to Denmark in the south by the Öresund Bridge, the longest combined road and rail bridge in Europe.

CENTRAL EUROPE

Central Europe is the region lying between the defined areas of Eastern and Western Europe. It includes the countries of Estonia, Latvia, Lithuania, Poland, Slovakia, Czech Republic and Hungary.

Czech Republic

The Czech Republic consists of the regions of Moravia and Bohemia. Moravia is mostly hills and lowlands and lies to the east; Bohemia is more of a plateau and is surrounded by mountains. The castles and palaces in the country are a wonderful attraction to tourists.

CZECH REPUBLIC
Capital: Prague
Area: 77,276 sq/km
Climate: temperate
Population: 10.2 million

The Tatra mountains form a natural border between Poland and Slovakia.

Prague

HUNGARY
Capital: Budapest
Area: 92,340 sq/km
Climate: temperate
Population: 10 million

Budapest

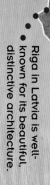

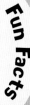

Warsaw

POLAND
Capital: Warsaw
Area: 304,459 sq/km
Climate: temperate to cold
Population: 38.5 million

Estonia

A republic in northeastern Europe on the Baltic Sea, Estonia is the smallest of the Baltic States. Curiously, it has the highest ratio of meteorite craters to land area in the world and it is also one of the most sparsely populated countries in Europe.

Vilnius

Riga

Riga in Latvia is well-known for its beautiful, distinctive architecture.

Tallinn

ESTONIA
Capital: Tallinn
Area: 43,211 sq/km
Climate: moderate winters, temperate summers
Population: 1.3 million

Hungary

The Danube River flows north to south and cuts **landlocked** Hungary almost in half. The Hungarians migrated from Asia more than a thousand years ago. The culture is, thus, distinct from countries around it that are dominated by Germanic and Slavic peoples.

Fun Facts

The traditional houses in Slovakia, which are mostly wooden houses, are painted with designs based on traditional embroidery from the region.

SOUTHEASTERN EUROPE

The Balkan region in southeastern Europe takes its name from the Balkan Mountains, which run from Bulgaria into eastern Serbia.

Romania

On the Black Sea coast of southeastern Europe lies the country of Romania. The country is divided into three major regions — Wallachia in the south, Moldavia in the northeast, and Transylvania at the centre. Though the majority of the population is Romanian, there is a fair population of Hungarians too.

Greece

People have lived in Greece for more than 5,000 years. Its civilisation started about 2,500 years ago. The country of Greece has many islands. Some of its earlier people wrote plays that are still performed today. Greece is also known for its sculptures.

Fun Facts

The ancient ritual of barefooted dancing on smouldering embers, emerged in several remote villages in the Strandzha Mountains, in Bulgaria.

Slovenia

Slovenia is a state in central Europe and was once a part of Yugoslavia. Slovenia won its independence in June 1991, after a ten-day battle with the Yugoslav army. Of all the independent nations of the former Yugoslavia, Slovenia is the most prosperous, with the highest living standards.

ROMANIA
Capital: Bucharest
Area: 230,340 sq/km
Climate: temperate
Population: 22.2 million

CROATIA
Capital: Zagreb
Area: 56,414 sq/km
Climate: **Mediterranean** and **continental**
Population: 4.5 million

BULGARIA
Capital: Sofia
Area: 110,550 sq/km
Climate: temperate
Population: 7.2 million

GREECE
Capital: Athens
Area: 130,800 sq/km
Climate: temperate
Population: 10.7 million

The Bran castle is a national monument of Romania.

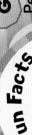

The Parthenon in Athens, Greece.

Bucharest

Sofia

Belgrade

Sarajevo

Tirane

Zagreb

Athens

NORTH AFRICA

Africa is the world's second-largest and second most-populated continent after Asia. North Africa is the northernmost region of the African continent, separated from the rest of Africa by the Sahara Desert.

Egypt

Egypt is one of the most populated countries in Africa and the Middle East. A great majority of the people live near the banks of the River Nile. Egypt is famous for its ancient civilisation and some of the world's most famous monuments, including the pyramid of Giza and its Great Sphinx. The terrain is dominated by deserts. The east is home to mountainous deserts, and the west has a drier desert. The Sahara lies to the south.

Rabat

Tripoli

LIBYA
Capital: Tripoli
Area: 1.75 million sq/km
Climate: Mediterranean to dry
Population: 6.3 million

Dakar

Abuja

Fun Facts

Although it is situated in North Africa, Morocco is the only African country that is presently not a member of the African Union.

Camel trekking in North Africa.

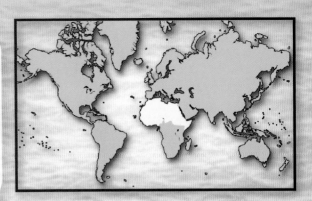

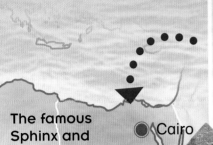

EGYPT
Capital: Cairo
Area: 995,450 sq/km
Climate: desert
Population: 83 million

The famous Sphinx and pyramids, Egypt.

○ Cairo

Sudan

Much of Sudan is a hot, dry place where nomads herd camels and sheep. Sudan's traditional dress, the jalabia, is a loose fitting robe well suited to desert conditions. It is usually worn with a large scarf and a thobe, which is a type of long shirt.

○ Khartoum

SUDAN
Capital: Khartoum
Area: 2.38 million sq/km
Climate: tropical to desert
Population: 41 million

Addis Ababa

Libya

Libya is blessed with oil, but it lacks water. It is the country with the highest per capita income in the continent. The population is mainly concentrated in its two major cities, Tripoli and Banghazi. Libya's Great Man-Made River Project is the biggest of its kind in the world, helping the **coastal** cities get much-needed water.

ETHIOPIA
Capital: Addis Ababa
Area: 1.12 million sq/km
Climate: tropical monsoon
Population: 85 million

DID YOU KNOW?

Ethiopia is Africa's largest coffee producing country and the second largest producer of cut flowers in Africa.

CENTRAL AND SOUTHERN
AFRICA

Central Africa is the heart of the African continent. It includes Burundi, the Central African Republic, Chad, Republic of the Congo, and Rwanda. Southern Africa consists of the Republic of South Africa, Zimbabwe and Namibia.

Burundi

This small nation is located southeast of the equator. Though small in size, it has a dense population. Agriculture is the dominant occupation, with 90 per cent of the population being farmers.

South Africa

The Republic of South Africa is a country located at the southern tip of the continent of Africa. South Africa is known for its great diversity in cultures, languages, religious beliefs and ethnic groups. For many years South Africa had a system of Apartheid, where racial groups were separated, but this was abolished in 1994, to great celebration worldwide.

REPUBLIC OF THE CONGO
Capital: Brazzaville
Area: 341,500 sq/km
Climate: tropical
Population: 4 million

Fun Facts

The country of Rwanda has a hill-dominated landscape. Because of this, it is nicknamed the 'land of a thousand hills'.

DID YOU KNOW?

The presence of important minerals like cobalt, copper, diamonds, gold, silver, tin and coltan makes the Congo one of Africa's most mineral-rich countries.

CHAD
Capital: Ndjamena
Area: 1.25 million sq/km
Climate: tropical and desert
Population: 10.3 million

Ndjamena

Chad

Chad is a landlocked nation with a diverse landscape. An arid centre and a desert-dominated north sit alongside the fertile south.
Chad has had an unstable few decades – primarily due to tension between the Arab-Muslim north and east and the African-Christian south.

The Congo is rich in its wildlife.

Brazzaville

The African lion is mostly found in southeast Africa.

Luanda

The semi-nomadic Masaai can be found in Tanzania and Kenya.

ANGOLA
Capital: Luanda
Area: 124 million sq/km
Climate: diverse (semi-arid to hot)
Population: 12.8 million

Harare

Pretoria

Maputo

SOUTH AFRICA
Capital: Pretoria
Area: 1.21 million sq/km
Climate: mostly semi-arid
Population: 49 million

MIDDLE EAST

The Middle East spans the whole of southwestern Asia and northeastern Africa. It has a dry and hot climate. Countries in the Middle East include Iraq, Iran, Israel, UAE, Kuwait and Jordan.

The Western, or Wailing Wall is one of the most sacred places for people of Jewish faith.

Jeruselam

Amman

ISRAEL
Capital: Jeruslam
Area: 20,330 sq/km
Climate: temperate
Population: 7.2 million

JORDAN
Capital: Amman
Area: 91,971 sq/km
Climate: mostly arid
Population: 6.3 million

Iran

Iran is a country full of mountains and deserts. Desert areas dominate the east of the country. Farming is primarily concentrated in the narrow plains or valleys in the north and west – places more likely to get rainfall. The oil reserves lie in the southwest.

Mecca is considered the centre of the Islamic faith.

Israel

The eastern interior of Israel is dry and includes the lowest point on the Earth's surface – the Dead Sea. The majority of the population is Jewish, with a minority Arab population.

Fun Facts

Iran is one of the world's oldest continuous major civilisations, with historical and urban settlements dating back to 4,000 BC.

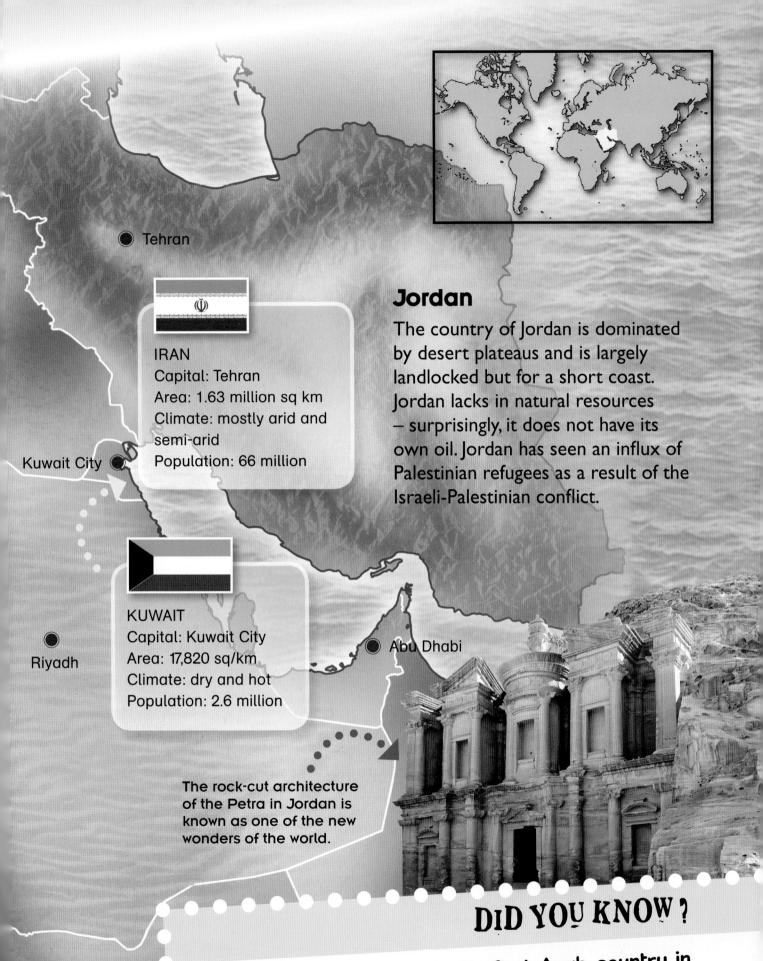

Tehran

IRAN
Capital: Tehran
Area: 1.63 million sq km
Climate: mostly arid and semi-arid
Population: 66 million

Kuwait City

Jordan

The country of Jordan is dominated by desert plateaus and is largely landlocked but for a short coast. Jordan lacks in natural resources – surprisingly, it does not have its own oil. Jordan has seen an influx of Palestinian refugees as a result of the Israeli-Palestinian conflict.

KUWAIT
Capital: Kuwait City
Area: 17,820 sq/km
Climate: dry and hot
Population: 2.6 million

Riyadh

Abu Dhabi

The rock-cut architecture of the Petra in Jordan is known as one of the new wonders of the world.

DID YOU KNOW ?

Kuwait was the first Arab country in the Gulf to have an elected parliament.

RUSSIA AND NEIGHBOURING COUNTRIES

Russia is the largest country in the world in terms of area. Its neighbours include Kazakhstan, Turkmenistan, Ukraine, Moldova, and Uzbekistan, among others.

The St. Basil's Cathedral is about 450 years old.

Moscow

The majestic but endangered Siberian tiger.

RUSSIA
Capital: Moscow
Area: 16.99 million sq/km
Climate: Diverse (warm to extremely cold)
Population: 140 million

Russia

Founded in the 12th century, Russia established worldwide power and influence to become the largest socialist state and a recognised superpower. Russia has many attractions, from freshwater lakes, soaring mountains, rivers and forests to beautiful and rich wildlife.

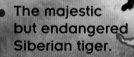

KAZAKHSTAN
Capital: Astana
Area: 2.66 million sq/km
Climate: continental
Population: 15.3 million

Kazakh people can be found in China and Mongolia as well.

Astana

UZBEKISTAN
Capital: Tashkent
Area: 425,400 sq/km
Climate: hot summers, mild winters
Population: 27.5 million

Bishkek

Tashkent

Kazakhstan

Kazakhstan is a country in central Asia and Eastern Europe. It is ranked as the ninth largest country in the world as well as the world's largest landlocked country. Kazakhstan is famous for the Baykonur Cosmodrome or space station.

Uzbekistan

Uzbekistan is central Asia's most populated nation. About 80 per cent of the country is dominated by the Qizilqum desert, with mountain ranges present in the southeast and the northeast of the country. The Fergana Valley lies to the country's northeast and is its most developed and fertile region, containing many industries.

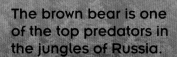
The brown bear is one of the top predators in the jungles of Russia.

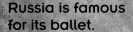
Russia is famous for its ballet.

Fun Facts

The Voronya Cave, situated in Georgia, is the deepest known cave in the world.

DID YOU KNOW?

Armenia is home to a leading centre of metallurgy, the scientific study of metal and its properties.

CHINA AND NEIGHBOURING COUNTRIES

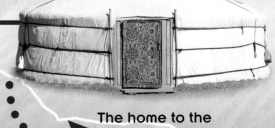

Ulan Bator ◉

The home to the nomadic Mongol.

China is the most populous country in the world and one of the biggest. Its neighbours include Japan, Singapore, Mongolia and Cambodia, among others.

China

China is the third largest country in the world. It is also one of the world's oldest civilisations with a history of more than 7,000 years. The landscape is diverse, with hills, plains, mountains, and deltas. The climate ranges from hot tropical in the south to subarctic in the northeast.

CHINA
Capital: Beijing
Area: 9.32 million sq/km
Climate: diverse
(tropical to very cold)
Population: 1.3 billion

Paddy fields — a feature of rice-growing China.

Fun Facts

Mongolia is the seventh largest country in Asia in terms of area. The country is totally landlocked, with China on one side and Russia on the other.

South Korea

South Korea comprises the southern half of the Korean peninsula, and numerous islands off the southern and western coasts. The landscape is full of mountains, though less in number than in North Korea.

China's great wall can be seen from the moon.

Beijing

P'yongyang

Seoul

JAPAN
Capital: Tokyo
Area: 374,744 sq/km
Climate: tropical to cool
Population: 127 million

Tokyo

SOUTH KOREA
Capital: Seoul
Area: 98,190 sq/km
Climate: temperate
Population: 48 million

Shanghai

Taipei

Japan

Japan is an island country in East Asia. The ancient Japanese people believed theirs was the first land awakened by the rising sun. The Japanese call their land Nippon, meaning 'land of the rising sun'. It is believed that only 18 percent of Japan's land is suitable for **settlement**, which explains the over-populated cites!

DID YOU KNOW?

In the Gobi Desert of Mongolia fossilised dinosaur remains were found in 1920s, as well as the first dinosaur egg.

THE INDIAN SUBCONTINENT

The subcontinent comprises India, Pakistan, Nepal, Bhutan, Bangladesh and Sri Lanka.

Kabul

Islamabad

Beautiful mosques like this one are abundant in Pakistan.

New Delhi

PAKISTAN
Capital: Islamabad
Area: 778,720 sq/km
Climate: mostly hot
Population: 176 million

The Taj Mahal is one of India's most beautiful monuments.

Mumbai

India

India is the biggest country in the subcontinent and has the second largest population in the world. India's physical, religious and racial variety is reflected in its culture. This vast cultural diversity is reflected in its religious **monuments** – temples, mosques, churches, monasteries, gurudwaras etc.

INDIA
Capital: New Delhi
Area: 2.97 million sq/km
Climate: tropical monsoon to temperate
Population: 1.1 billion

Chennai

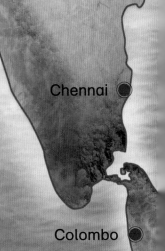

Colombo

Pakistan

The eastern and southern parts of the country have the Indus River and its tributaries; most of the population is concentrated along these areas. West of the river, the land is dry and mountainous. To the north lies K2, the tallest mountain in the world after Everest.

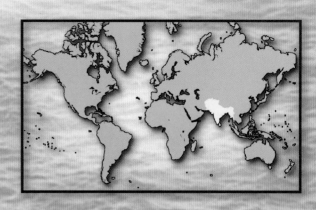

Fun Facts

Many of the houses in Bangladesh are often raised on stilts or embankments to help protect them from flooding.

Sri Lanka

Sri Lanka is a tropical island nation that lies at the southernmost tip of India. Most of the well-renowned tea plantations are found at the centre of the country. The Sinhalese community constitutes the majority of the population, while the Tamils dominate the minority. The southwest is the most densely populated, and it is here that you can find Colombo, the country's capital.

Rickshaws are still a popular mode of transport in the subcontinent.

Dhaka

Kolkata

BANGLADESH
Capital: Dhaka
Area: 133,910 sq/km
Climate: tropical
Population: 156 million

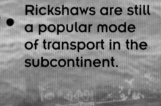

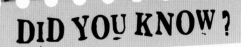

DID YOU KNOW?

Eight of the highest peaks of the world, including Mount Everest, are situated in Nepal.

SOUTHEAST ASIA

Southeast Asia lies south of China, east of India and north of Australia. The region is known for earthquakes and tremors (seismic activity) because several geological plates meet here.

Hanoi

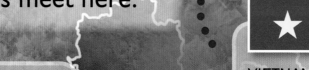

VIETNAM
Capital: Hanoi
Area: 325,360 sq/km
Climate: diverse (tropical to dry)
Population: 87 million

THAILAND
Capital: Bangkok
Area: 511,770 sq/km
Climate: tropical
Population: 66 million

Thailand

The Chao Phraya River basin dominates the country of Thailand. Bangkok, the country's capital, lies in this basin. East Thailand is mainly woodlands and grasses. The southern region is full of hills and is well forested. Northern Thailand has the highest mountains.

Bangkok

Phnom Penh

The Petronas Towers are two of the tallest buildings in the world.

MALAYSIA
Capital: Kuala Lumpur
Area: 328,550 sq/km
Climate: tropical
Population: 26 million

Kuala Lumpur

116

Vietnam

Vietnam is 1,600 km (1,000 miles) long from north to south and is extremely narrow – just 40 km (25 miles) wide at its narrowest. The Red River and the Mekong River dominate the landscape. Hanoi is the main city of the Red River, and Ho Chi Minh is the main city of the Mekong River.

Cambodia

Cambodia is mostly covered with forests. Once a war zone in the latter half of the 20th century, the country enjoys greater stability these days. **Subsistence farming** is still the predominant means of earning.

Manila

The Petronas Towers in Malaysia are the world's tallest twin buildings and were the tallest buildings in the world until Taipei 101 was built.

An exotic Bali dancer.

DID YOU KNOW?

Indonesia is a transcontinental country spanning Southeast Asia and Oceania, comprised of more than 17,000 islands!

AUSTRALIA AND NEIGHBOURING COUNTRIES

Australia is a country in the southern hemisphere. Australasian countries include New Zealand, East Timor, Solomon Islands and Papua New Guinea.

Settlement in Australia

Aboriginal settlers arrived on the continent from Southeast Asia about 40,000 years before the first Europeans began exploration in the 17th century. Six colonies were created in the late 18th and 19th centuries. Today, Australia is one of the most popular destinations for tourists.

Papua New Guinea

Papua New Guinea, in the Southwest Pacific, is one of the most diverse countries in the world. This largely unexplored nation has over 850 indigenous languages.

AUSTRALIA
Capital: Canberra
Area: 7.6 million sq/km
Climate: arid to semi-arid
Population: 21 million

The red kangaroo is the national animal of Australia.

Perth

DID YOU KNOW

The world's largest saltwater lagoon, Marovo Lagoon, is situated in New Georgia, Solomon Islands.

PAPUA NEW GUINEA
Capital: Port Morseby
Area: 452,860 sq/km
Climate: tropical
Population: 6 million

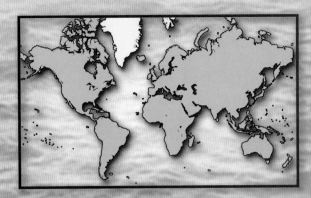

SOLOMON ISLANDS
Capital: Honiara
Area: 27,540 sq/km
Climate: tropical monsoon
Population: 600,000

Rugby, the country's national game, is followed passionately in New Zealand.

The Sydney Opera House stages up to 2,500 art performances and events each year.

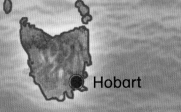

Sydney

Canberra

Melbourne

Hobart

New Zealand

New Zealand is an island country in the south-western Pacific Ocean. It has two main landmasses, the North Island and the South Island, and numerous smaller islands. The original Maori inhabitants named New Zealand Aotearoa, meaning 'the land of the long white cloud'. The indigenous, flightless kiwi is the country's national bird.

NEW ZEALAND
Capital: Wellington
Area: 268,021 sq/km
Climate: temperate
Population: 4.2 million

Wellington

THE POLES AND GREENLAND

The Earth, like a magnet, has two poles – the North Pole and the South Pole. These regions are dominated by the polar ice-caps, resting on the Arctic Ocean and the continent of Antarctica.

North Pole

The Earth's North Pole is covered by a floating pack of ice over the Arctic Ocean. The land from the North Pole down to the northern forests is known as the Tundra. Despite the extreme climate, animals that survive and make the Tundra their home include polar bears, Arctic hares and Arctic foxes.

The fur of the Arctic fox turns grey-brown during summer.

The polar bear is an accomplished swimmer and is often found at sea.

GREENLAND
Capital: Nuuk
Area: 2.16 million sq/km
Climate: extreme cold
Population: 57,600

South Pole

The landmass of the Earth's South Pole (or Antarctica) is covered by the Antarctic ice sheet. Seventy per cent of the fresh water on Earth can be found in this ice sheet. The South Pole is much colder than the North Pole as it receives less solar radiation.

Greenland

Greenland is one of the world's largest island, but it is not classified as a continent. Geographically a part of North America, its history is dominated by Denmark, Norway and Iceland.

The penguin is one of the few living creatures thriving in the Antarctic.

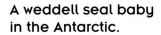

A weddell seal baby in the Antarctic.

Fun Facts

There are no permanent human residents in Antarctica because of the freezing cold.

DID YOU KNOW

Less rain falls annually in Antarctica than in the Sahara Desert!

GLOSSARY

Adapt: to change according to the situation and circumstance

Endangered: something that is in danger of vanishing from the Earth

Gills: respiratory organ of animals that live in water

Hump: something that bulges out

Migrate: move from one region to another

Nocturnal: animals that are active during the night

Offspring: babies; the young of an animal

Predator: animal that hunts

Primate: an animal group that includes monkeys

Self defence: to protect oneself

Serrated: having a row of sharp, saw-like teeth

Venom: poisonous substance secreted by some animals

Vibration: move back and forth in a rapid manner

Asteroids: floating rocks in space that move around the Sun

Axis: imaginary line around which the Earth rotates

Camouflage: disguise

Dense: something thick where very little light can pass through

Equator: imaginary line around the centre of the Earth

Evolution: process by which something changes over time

Excretion: process of discharging unnecessary waste matter from the body

Earthquake: shaking and vibration of the Earth's surface

Gravity: force of attraction

GLOSSARY

between two bodies

Hemisphere: Half of the Earth – divided into Southern and Northern Hemispheres

Photosynthesis: process by which plants use sunlight to make their food

Reproduction: process of producing young, by birth or other method

Shoreline: boundary between water and land

Biodiversity: range of plants and animals living in a specific area

Coastal: relating to or of a coast

Continental: something typical of mainland Europe

Diverse: different and many

Earth: planet where we live

Himalayas: a 2,400 km (1,500 mile) mountain range in India and Tibet

Indigenous: originating where it was found

Landlocked: surrounded by land

Landscape: all the visible features of an area

Mediterranean: related to or near the Mediterranean Sea

Monuments: historical structures

Natural Resource: resources found in nature

Rockies: mountain range of western North America

Settlement: area where a group of people live together

Subsistence farming: farming that produces food enough for a farmer's family

INDEX

INDEX